A
MOTHER'S
SPACE

Dear Rebecca
Thank you for all
you do to bring spiritual
awareness to the world!
I hope you enjoy this book
and that it might
resonate with your current
stage of life & motherhood!

A MOTHER'S SPACE

Permission to Pause

TEHLA JANE BOWER

A catalogue record for this book is available from the National Library of Australia.

Trade Paperback ISBN: 978-0-6455978-2-0
eBook ISBN: 978-0-6455978-3-7

We at The Kind Press acknowledge that Aboriginal and Torres Strait Islander peoples are the Traditional Custodians and the first storytellers of the lands on which we live and work; and we pay our respects to Elders past and present.

THE
KIND
PRESS

www.thekindpress.com

For the mother desperately longing for a peaceful pause in her day.
This book is dedicated to you.

The author acknowledges the Bundjalung, Dharawal, Yuin and Ngarabal peoples as the Traditional Custodians of the lands on which this book has been written. She recognises their knowledge and continuing connection to the land, waterways and native wildlife; and pays her respect to Elders past, present and emerging. She extends this respect to all First Nations peoples across the land.

CONTENTS

PART THREE: DEEPER DISCOVERING

A NOTE FOR YOU, DEAR READER

Beautiful Reader,

I am going to make an intuitive assumption that if you are reading this book, you might be seeking something. It may not be something you can put words to. It could simply be a feeling, or a yearning, a grasping of something from your past that you cannot quite reach back to. You can almost put your finger on it and then your baby starts crying, or your toddler hurtles towards the stairs, or the sibling in-fighting starts up for the tenth time in a row. What was that inkling of a feeling that passed by just before? If only you had a free moment to process it.

You might feel you do not even have time to read to the end of this sentence. But please, stay with me. For this story is about someone else who knows of this 'seeking feeling', someone who has spent a good chunk of a decade trying to carefully slice out a slither of space for herself each day to investigate this feeling further.

Let me tell you a bit more about her and why she is here. Each day, she tries her best to navigate through the wild mess and tangle of the sticky web of motherhood, like hundreds of millions around the world just like her. Snapped to attention by increasing moments of fatigue, guilt and despair, she chooses to use her life as an experiment of sorts, trialling this and testing that, with the goal of finding herself at peace again. She craves to feel worthy and confident once more and lit up by little moments that belong only to her. She cherishes these moments like a conversation with an old and dear friend. It is here she starts to listen to the quiet whisperings of encouragement and reassurance making their way lovingly into her ear, helping to guide her and reinforce the importance of this time. As she starts to query the accepted ways of doing things, she probes around the pockets of her brain for possible alternatives.

What if I did send my toddler to day-care, even if it's not a workday, just to give myself a well-deserved break for my own wellbeing?

What if I could sit and drink my entire cup of coffee in one go, before it curdles and turns stone cold. How would that feel?

What if I dared sneak off to the movies all by myself, just once?

What if the solution is not just a boozy annual girls' weekend away that I have to wait all year for, but the creation of a small spoonful of space in my day—every day?

What if …
What if …
What if …

Can you relate? Are you nodding your head knowingly? Do you crave someone to recognise your deep desire to break away for a breath? You are not alone. This book was written for you and is dedicated to you. It honours you and all you have sacrificed. It equips you with all the encouragement you need to respect your quiet inner voice and reserve space for yourself without feeling guilty.

THE STORY OF THE MOTHER

I am Tehla, the author of this book, and my writing confesses my raw experiments with seeking out quiet spaces in my day as a mother. It includes all the challenges and pitfalls as well as the golden nuggets of joy when I succeed in my endeavours.

It is my story, but it is yours too. I hope I can be that gentle guide at your side cheering you on as you find your own slice of space with ease and grace.

Are you ready?

INTRODUCTION

This book has been in the pipeline for just over a decade. That's the same length of time as my entire thirties—plus one year! And the age of my precious eldest daughter—eleven years.

I started scratching out a few words one weekday in 2012 when she was nine months old. My husband and I had been getting on each other's nerves all that week. I was struggling to keep my eyes open from endless sleepless nights and a baby who had already cut out her daytime sleep. Yes, at nine months of age! Also, a new strong emotion was bubbling to the surface I can now clearly identify as guilt. The effect this had on me was profound and confusing.

I remember flopping down at a café inside a busy shopping centre overwhelmed by exhaustion and emotion, baby by my side. I distracted her with a pram full of plush playthings and teething rusks, enough to grant me time to pull out my notebook and pen.

I scribbled passionately and illegibly, trying to make sense of my new role as a mother. I drew pictures and diagrams only I could understand. I mapped out all my states of mind contributing to the eventual explosion of emotion at its peak. The page looked like an angry volcano.

It was enough to ignite something deep within my blood. My story began.

With bleeding nipples, painful haemorrhoids and a ringworm (on my face!), I lamented my load and took stock of my current life situation.

- Stress, enervation and agitation engulfed me
- I felt empty, lost and alone
- I felt society had somehow 'cheated' me by not revealing the 'real' state of motherhood
- I was bubbling with resentment that my husband could carry on in his professional life while I was stuck figuring this out on my own
- I didn't know who I was anymore
- I wanted a magic fairy to come wave her wand and take me to a time where I was back in control of my life again, joyful and carefree!

In that moment, I committed to offering up my own life as an experiment, as an alternative to wallowing in self-pity and misery. I grappled my guilt to the ground and poked my tongue out at it. Every time I found myself making excuses about why I couldn't leave my baby with my partner or family member for an hour, I visualised the guilt vanishing from under my feet. Creating space for myself as a mother became a clear priority in my life. So, I have spent the past decade writing, researching and documenting my investigations in 'space-seeking'. Eleven years later, I am excited to share my findings with the mothers who need to hear it.

A Mother's Space: Permission to Pause is a teaching memoir that chronicles my own story as a new mother struggling to find a small pocket of space in my day to reclaim my spirit and sanity, a personal and spiritual time that belongs only to me. My story encourages you to try it for yourself—one micro moment at a time.

The cliché of a long bubble bath and a massage doesn't cut it anymore. We need an updated formula for self-care which is nurturing and relatable, but also attainable within the time-poverty so many of us experience.

A Mother's Space is not a self-help book, nor is it another how-to-parent-your-child book. In fact, the focus is squarely on you. It argues that what we need as mothers is sacred moments of space in our day, every day, to make us feel human and held. This book equips you with all the encouragement you need to respect your quiet inner voice and reserve space for yourself without the nip of guilt on your heels.

The original title for this book was '*My Mummy-Life Crisis*', a big, scary headline that represented the equally bold and overwhelming phase of motherhood I found myself drowning in at the time. It was like an early version of a mid-life crisis, featuring a tiny human being who could not survive without me. I was a boiling pot of anxiety, angst, exhaustion and depletion. I was malnourished, sleep deprived and on the cusp of being diagnosed with a debilitating thyroid disease. I would have given anything to have a scientifically proven explanation to explain the irrational behaviour I was exerting. *Hello, Matrescence! Where were you and your delicious definitions all those years ago?*

If I could have magicked the words to come together at that point, this version of the book would have taken you on a wild rampage into the jungle of early motherhood with an abundance of expletives and a lack of direction and focus, leaving you just as dazed and confused as I was. Instead, I've included an opening passage at the start of the book as a legacy to this phase. It is appropriately titled *'Cracked Open: The Mummy Life Crisis that Saved Me'* and I hope it doesn't scare you off too much!

With a halo of hindsight now floating luminously over my head, I have a few more years up my sleeve and have softened my initial approach. I no longer desire a silver bullet to explain and fix everything. I'm done with baffling, detailed diagrams on whiteboards trying to predict and analyse my life. I have surrendered efforts to control each and every waking moment of my day. I have exchanged my busy career life for a slower, healthier and more balanced working lifestyle, and we have moved our little family away from metropolitan life to a beautiful coastal community. I am content to monotask instead of unsuccessfully multitasking my way through my day.

Slowly. Softly. Intentionally. Purposefully.

The first section of this book is called *'The Clearing'*. Like a mammoth spring-cleaning session, it is the phase of preparation and upheaval required to invite more space into your life. Guilt, identity, relationships, technology demands and domestics are all obstacles that block you from accessing your well-deserved personal space. I call them 'space-blockers'.

How many times have you fantasised about a peaceful morning or afternoon to yourself, or about signing up to a workshop or retreat you know you would love, only to be talked out of it as soon as the thought-bubble popped into your head?

Once we experience 'the clearing' in our lives we give ourselves permission to consider a new approach to prioritising our own desires for space. We can open ourselves up to fresh opportunities without the stigma of society and the perception of what we 'should be' doing breathing down our necks. Flick it to the curb. This, my friend, is The Clearing.

'The Discovering', the second part of this book, is dedicated to sharing the discoveries I made once I cleared the way for space to seep into my life. The creation of a sacred area in my home that belonged only to me, my quest for a hot cup of tea that wasn't microwaved ten times, a quiet space for grieving the loss of loved ones, a profound meditation on a rock at the beach, a digital detox. I embraced my newly discovered curiosity about how I could carve out five minutes here and five minutes there to sustain myself beyond just 'surviving' this parenting gig. I wanted to enjoy rather than endure the sacred role of motherhood by looking out for my own wellbeing in the same way I would for anyone else in my family.

'Deeper Discovering', the third and final part of this book, is about being confident in my endeavours to find time for myself. A solo hike with a kookaburra and a mouse, a half-day adventure into a spiritual oasis, a night away on my own. If it turned into five hours here and there, or an overnight escapade then so be it! I ultimately realised what I needed was a set of simple, practical ways to find peace every day, a pocket of personal space that could be accessed on tap, if and when the opportunity arose. After a decade of parenting, I have learned it is in these quieter, reflective and spiritual moments of pause that I can ultimately free myself from the grasps of guilt, doubt and self-sabotage. That in this layer of my life, my space as a mother is revered and meaningful, providing me with purpose and permission to inexcusably be myself. In essence, I have become a 'space seeker'. This doesn't mean I don't love spending time with my children. It means that if I don't get some breathing space to look after myself every now and then, I won't be the best version of myself nor a role model for my girls.

It is likely that if you are reading this book, you may not have the luxury of perusing it from start to finish in a nice, neat little sitting. Know that this is perfectly okay. This book is deliberately structured for you to pick it up, choose a chapter that grabs your interest and read it bite-size at your leisure. Each chapter concludes with a thought provoking 'pause prompt' and inspiring affirmation to support you along your journey. These prompts summarise the key themes of the chapter, so if you are light on time, skip straight to them.

Treat this as your daily oracle, or dive in deeper when you find longer stretches of time.

It is here, waiting, when you are ready.

The ultimate aim of writing this book is to not only share my own personal experiences. I want to reveal to mothers everywhere that it is possible to carve out a little bit of time and space for yourself every day. If I can do it, you can! I've always been someone who loves to learn by doing. This book is the accumulation of trial and error, highs and lows and spontaneous spikes of exuberance. I invite you to share in my story and experiences and take what you need to implement opportunities for space-salvation in your own life.

> Think of it as an essential facet of your family's health insurance. Everyone benefits from a contented mother who is less stressed and filled with passion and purpose.

Thank you for allowing me to share my story and ideas with you. My hope is this book inspires and encourages you to carve out your own space with confidence, conviction and grace. It is your permission slip for surrender and space and to pause in your day. You are worthy of it, and you absolutely deserve it!

Motherhood has made me question myself, doubt myself and love myself more than anything else in my forty-two years on this planet. Sometimes, it restricts my breath and fills me with so much fear of the world around me. Other times, it stops me in my tracks altogether and forces me to focus only on the most important things in this life. And, often times, I am so bloody exhausted that my appreciation for 'me' time becomes so immense that I look after myself in ways I never would have bothered to in the past. This is the cornerstone of *A Mother's Space: Permission to Pause* and I cannot wait to share it with you.

Tehla Jane xx

CRACKED OPEN: THE MUMMY LIFE CRISIS THAT SAVED ME

"The best thing about rock bottom is the rock part.
You discover the solid bit of you.
The bit that can't be broken down further.
The thing that you might sentimentally call a soul."

Matt Haig

As an expectant mother in the first half of 2011, I bubbled with preconceptions. *Would I be a natural mum? How would I know what to do with such a tiny human when she finally entered the world? Would she like me?*

The questions whorled around my head as I flopped exhausted into bed in my final trimester of pregnancy. *Would childbirth be as painful as I imagined it to be? Would we get any sleep at all once she was born? Would I return to work after six months as I had so confidently proclaimed I would? Would I be a good mum? Would I change?*

Like most first-time mothers, my list of questions was enough to fill an entire collection of Encyclopaedia Britannica's. There was, however, one aspect of motherhood I did not anticipate or predict.

I did not foresee the dramatic diminishment of my
own time, my sacred space, my own company
with my own thoughts and just how much of an
impact this would have on my quality of life.

Where did my private space go? Why was it so important that I continued to have it? And why on earth did I feel so selfish and embarrassed for even recognising this?

New questions popped into my head. *How could I reserve some space for myself each day that could be mine and mine alone? Was there a certain time of day I could squeeze it in and make it routine?*

At nine months post-birth, my immense joy and excitement was counterbalanced with a sheer lack of 'me' time.

During this inaugural initiation period of
motherhood, I felt like I was at my baby's every
beck and call. My boobs were just as exhausted as
I was in meeting the constant feeding demands of
this new little human in our lives, despite being at
their most impressive size of all time.

I only hoped it got easier. Every single person I bumped into assured me it would. I had been in business and professional roles for the past decade, but nothing I had learned in my academic or career life could be applied to this demanding new role. The long hours of writing funding submissions for my clients now seemed a piece of cake in comparison.

Could there actually be some logical sense to this vicious cycle and wonderful mess of motherhood?

THE YEAR THAT BROKE AND THEN SAVED ME

Unfortunately, I didn't have much time to mull it over. I fell pregnant with my second child just as I was getting my head around the ups and downs, ebbs and flows of first-time motherhood. My second daughter, Avah, came along when Kahlan, my first, was two and a half years old. By no fault of her own, it was the start of a string of ongoing sicknesses and health issues. As a newborn, Avah was admitted to hospital at two weeks old with bronchiolitis, followed in close succession by a glue ear diagnosis, ruptured eardrums and surgery at eight months old. She was one of our Ear Nose and Throat (ENT) doctor's youngest patients to get grommets. Our specialist was kind enough to fit both our daughters in for grommet surgery within weeks of each other, just days before the Christmas of 2014. It was a summer to remember.

The girls were fitted out in their ear-strap headbands made from wetsuit material and Velcro to protect their ears every time they went near a drop of water—beach, pool and even their nightly bath! The risk of water reaching the middle ear was high and, if it got in, would result in the administering of drops of hydrogen peroxide into the ear canal. This was followed by plunging a finger into the ear as a suction, resulting in a bubbling and fizzing sound of success as the debris were drawn out. The long-term side effects of this remedy often woke me up at night, if I happened to be sleeping in the first place!

I became an unofficial expert on everything paediatric-ear-related—infection, rupture, hearing tests, respiratory conditions and pain relief. I knew every idiosyncrasy of the reception ladies and surgeons at the ENT surgery rooms. The waiting times. The payment systems. The phoneline that never connected when I called in a panic. The lightning speed of speech of our specialist, leaving me feel like the words had been vacuumed into my brain and scrambled into a storm of confusion. Our visits were so predictable, yet so stressful.

My childhood friend Bessie was the only other person in my network going through a similar ear regime. I held onto our texts, messages and phone conversations with sheer relief that someone else understood and related to what we were going through.

In 2015, I found myself facing the new year with my own pressures as the main support engine for the wellbeing of my kids and my husband, who was completely burnt out from work. I developed a number of my own health issues, including TMJ and Hashimoto's Disease. I felt I couldn't move fast enough through the day to keep everyone happy. I neglected myself to the point where my body literally and physically shut down.

Shortly after my Hashimoto's diagnosis, Avah, now aged seventeen months, was hospitalised with pneumonia. The four days I spent by her bedside, watching her little body struggle for breath, broke me into a million pieces. Each morning when the paediatric doctors did their rounds, they stood huddled together armed with clipboards and concerned expressions on their faces as their eyes stole glances in and out of Avah's room.

At the exact same time, Kahlan, aged three, was diagnosed with scarlet fever after a lump the size of a golf ball popped out of her neck. I wish I was exaggerating, but it was so huge her head was asymmetrical. The rage I exhibited towards the doctor at our medical centre was unacceptable in hindsight, however I felt justified at the time. It had taken five visits and numerous turn aways before they agreed to test her. I know you won't need convincing when I say that a mother's intuition is always right. My youngest daughter's life is a testament to that. I was wrung out, strung out and desperate to get my girls better so I could focus on fixing myself.

A few months later, the girls recovered. I finally felt confident we wouldn't be making any more midnight trips up to the emergency unit at the hospital, so I booked in to my first silent meditation retreat at the local Buddhist temple. I learned so much about myself during this time that I started to truly believe in myself and take control of my destiny in my own way. I learnt how to 'monotask' as opposed to multitask and how to meditate with tea, through the fascinating Japanese practice of 'tea chan'. Importantly, I learnt to let go of stereotypes and stigmas and to just be myself. It was an absolute relief and weight off my shoulders.

'NOT WITHOUT MY JOURNAL'

Those brief pockets of stillness followed by sublime silence saved me from the brink of breakdown on multiple occasions. I recorded as much detail as possible in my trusty little handbag journal. Two minutes of scribbling here, five minutes there. I surrendered to my role as a mother and took whatever little snippets of time I could get to document this for future reference.

A journal entry from around this time recounted a morning where I gave myself permission to 'just be' despite the demands of work and household:

This morning I had the very rare chance to have the house to myself, so, instead of working, I decided to give myself the morning off, drop the kids at day-care and see where my desire took me.

It took me first to the coffee shop, then drove me to the little lighthouse where I took off my shoes. I walked barefoot, diary in hand, to the base of the lighthouse where I lay my head back and rested it against the sun-soaked cement. I closed my eyes.

I forgot about everything that needed to be done. I watched the pelicans interacting with each other. I smiled at the congregation of Chinese fishermen casting their lines off the break wall. And I became absorbed in the movement of the ocean as it caressed me, enticing me back into my own body and mind.

AN INTENTION TO SPONTANEOUSLY SURRENDER

I made a commitment to regularly and spontaneously surrender to the opportunities that presented themselves to me. Creating space for myself as a mother became a clear priority in my life. To never feel guilty for claiming this time, and to grab it even if it was a mere five to ten minutes here and there!

I said yes to opportunities that encouraged me to follow a new calling in my career and shift away from corporate life to spiritual health and wellness pursuits.

I am grateful I was pushed so hard into the ground that I never thought I'd be able to keep going. I am thankful for the health conditions that pivoted me away from stress and towards balance. I am so grateful to my precious girls for being my biggest teachers in this life. If it wasn't for the year that broke me, I would likely still be doing the same job, in the same town, with a workaholic husband and a 'my dreams can wait'/ 'it's not that bad' mindset.

And this book would never have been written.

Part 1
THE CLEARING

Chapter 1

Finding Space And
The Art Of Pick-Up Sticks

*"Sometimes, in the midst of bleeping screens, tiny hands
tugging at us with infinite needs, stories to craft, reports to
write, emails to hammer out, stomachs to fill, we need
to reach for tiny drops of stillness."*

Julia Baird

Every mother I know is stretched for space. The simple
art of drinking an entire cup of steaming tea or coffee in
one luscious sitting is a luxury. To wander the aisles of the
supermarket at 8.30pm exudes a freedom lost somewhere
between our third trimester ultrasound and the latch of babe
to breast or bottle. To drive alone in the car without cries from
the backseat or spew on our shoulder. Showering without
yelling, screaming or endless interruptions. Our own space.
Our own company. Most of us long for it with a quiet sense
of desperation laced with a meticulously woven basket of
sentimental longing.

And most of us have no idea *how* we can get it back.

I massaged my mind with this thought one Saturday
morning. Heating my takeaway coffee in the microwave for

the third time, I reflected on my own needs. I just needed to sit for five minutes in peace with my yoghurt, fruit and coffee. Just *five minutes* is really all I needed to clear my mind, silence my buzzing nervous system from an intense week and prepare myself for the next task. The kids were whingeing around my ankles, eating my half-consumed breakfast, breaking each other's Lego masterpieces and fighting over the dolly pram.

Something clicked in me, a panicked kind of pressure and internal knowing. In the calmest, most collected way possible, I heated my coffee for the fourth time, packed my breakfast into a Tupperware container, threw it into my handbag and announced to my husband that I was taking my breakfast 'offsite' for consumption. Before I could scan his face for criticism or hear the cries of my children objecting to my departure, I strapped myself safely into the driver's seat of my car and flung the gearstick into reverse. Off I went!

This fleeting, instinctive decision saved my morning.

As I sat perched on my rock at the harbour, I reflected on how similar my quest for personal space was to a game of pick-up sticks that had reached its final round. If I could carefully extract just one coloured stick from beneath the pile without moving any others, I could rejoice and high-five myself as I escaped out the door with a wide-brimmed grin on my face.

I have learned from these little moments of daring escapades that it is vital to listen to intuitive cues and take action before the situation eats you up and spits you out. This is not wrong. You do not need to feel guilty for giving yourself some time out.

These little pockets of space recharge you,
recentre you and polish the lens on your life.

Dedicating time and space to yourself is not always easy. But, like most things, the more you do of it, the easier it gets. My children don't always like it when I choose to spend time without them. But the more routine and regular you can make your alone time, the more they come to understand and respect that mummy's time is important to her. And there's no need to worry, she always comes back!

Some mothers seem to be more natural at prioritising their personal space than others. I am not one of them, and I assume you are not either if you were drawn to this book! In reality, it often depends on the level of support we have around us. To be able to take time out, you do need someone to fill the void when you're gone. This is especially so when caring for very young children.

A mother at my girls' school somehow manages to go for a long run and coffee with her running buddy before school most days. Another mum, who attends my yoga classes, gets up every day at 4.30 am to go to the gym before work. And no, she doesn't work in radio! There's also the mother from my family network who religiously gets her nails done every two weeks.

Creating space looks different for each of us. It
takes dedication, self-worth and commitment.
We need to be prepared to challenge our
contemporary calendar settings and social

status and prioritise our own health and personal needs—ideally at least once a day.

My eldest daughter was at least three years old before I finally realised that I couldn't do it on my own, especially when my second baby came along and was quite unwell for the first twelve months of her life.

I was so used to feeling in control all the time and I wasn't willing to hand the reins to someone else. When I did, even to my husband or my mum, I left pages of instructions with precise timings and more detail than the instruction manual for a light aircraft!

As mothers, we do not want for much. The 2016 film 'Bad Moms' sums it up so well: to eat breakfast uninterrupted on our own, to stop being pressured to be a perfect mother, to stop the judgements from other mothers, to encourage our children to help themselves by doing simple tasks like their own homework or making their own school lunches.

When we become mothers, we experience one of the greatest paradigm shifts of our lifetime. By recognising this and shifting with it, we can embrace the good and the bad, the highs and the lows, the shit sandwiches and the magical moments of sheer love and happiness. And we can release our unrealistic expectations of ourselves and simply surrender.

"The simple intention to surrender control is all you need to experience miracles."
Gabby Bernstein

Letting go and surrendering to yourself ensures you can look afresh at ways of claiming a bit of time for you. It involves surrendering to the tiny thrust of space in between puke and puree, poo and pee, sleepless sexless nights, irrational emotional tidal waves of joy and sadness, anger and frustration, sublime excitement and sheer exhaustion. That is okay. You are still there, nestled tightly within the chaos of your newfound family life. Our children might test us, but they also remind us how amazing we are, to have sacrificed our bodies, our freedom and our pre-existing lives to give them the best chance at life, at love, at existing in a way that we did, and our mothers did before us (thanks, Mum!).

PAUSE PROMPT
ASK YOURSELF OUT ON A DATE

Are you afraid to be in your own company? What emotions rise up when you read this? Is there an element of truth? As mothers, we forget how to be with ourselves because for many days, weeks and years, we are never alone. We say we crave alone time, but we become out of practise with walking into a café without a baby on our hip who everyone greets. Or going to a family event without a toddler to fill any awkward silences. Suddenly, we find ourselves alone with our own thoughts!

It's okay to admit you feel a little torn, craving space, but also missing your children desperately when you're not with them. Wanting to hear yourself think, but also not wanting to hear the thoughts that come up. This is why, especially in the early days of making space, it's good to give your alone time some structure.

Think of it as dating yourself.

When you first meet another person, you think about where you'll go, what you might do, what you might say. Do the same with yourself. Start by making a plan, think about where you'll be most comfortable, and set yourself up for success.

Push past the need to be with someone else or in a group 'doing' something. Be bold and courageous and set yourself free in your own company! Your soul will thank you for it.

Permission Note

I follow my desire for personal 'me' time by surrendering to spontaneous opportunities sprinkled throughout my day.

Chapter 2

Taming the Guilt to
Let Space In

"Guilt to mothers is like grapes to wine."

Fay Weldon

Scrubbing the house from top to toe, I was preparing for a forthcoming property inspection. Anticipating the real estate agent's arrival any minute, I muttered under my breath what a waste of my energy this cleaning and tidying was when I could be getting more important tasks done. How I despised housework!

To my surprise, the young agent arrived at my door looking just as dishevelled as I felt. No sooner had we exchanged pleasantries that she blurted out how exhausted she was, and in desperate need of a break from her fifteen-month-old son. A recently planned child-free weekend away had fallen through which would have been her first proper break since giving birth. She was feeling every minute and sleepless night of her sixty-week initiation into motherhood.

She went on to tell me how she had gratefully accepted an opportunity from her employer to leave early the Thursday afternoon prior. This early mark had enabled her to wander the shops freely, knowing she didn't have to pick her toddler up from day-care for another two hours. However, her immediate sense of freedom was snatched after a mere fifteen minutes by the chattering of her mind, smothering her loftiness with a noxious niggle in the centre of her chest.

It was, of course, the undesirable grapple of guilt.

'I started to think, oh, I shouldn't leave him there if I don't have to. It's such a long day for him and he'll be so tired. Maybe I should just go and collect him early so I can get him home and bathed and fed. But you wouldn't believe it. I got there to pick him up and he was having so much fun that he chucked an enormous tantrum and refused to come with me! I should have stayed at the shops wandering around!'

This story is like a dart thrown squarely into the bullseye of the board of guilt. It reveals how guilt grows and morphs within a mother, preying on the slightest whiff of her self-doubt and pouncing on her like a cheetah to a gazelle.

Hearing her story toggled a memory from my own vault of guilt when my girls were aged four and two. I took a work trip down to Melbourne for a three-day conference, so it was a longer timeframe than the story of my new real estate friend. After boarding in Sydney, I sat paralysed with a knot the size of a rock melon in my gut while the plane waited on the tarmac. A crushing sensation gradually took over the deep cavities of my chest and I realised I was on the verge of tears. A quick physical audit ruled out a panic (or heart!) attack and I almost laughed at the recognition of the culprit of these emotional and physical strains.

Guilt!

It took almost half the length of the flight before the grip of guilt released and fretting about leaving my baby at day-care with a runny nose eased. The look of misery on my four-year-old's face as her beautiful blue eyes bore a hole into my conscience remained a while longer. Of course, they were both fine in the safe care of my husband. Although I felt relief at this, it also ignited a mental discourse and subsequent analysis over why our male counterparts do not appear to be as plagued with guilt as we are. My husband had been away for much longer periods and regularly worked from 6.00 am to 8.30 pm or later every day, so why did I feel so bad?

Why did I feel so *undeserving* of this time?

Why do we, as mothers, feel so *unworthy* of this time?

When it comes to claiming some space to ourselves, guilt is one of the biggest factors inhibiting us from going through with it. It is likely *the* biggest of hurdles on the obstacle course as we circumnavigate the opportunity to grant ourselves some time out. What is it that is truly stopping us from drinking a hot cup of tea, or taking two minutes more in the shower, or—shock horror—taking a morning off just to connect with ourselves again?

GUILT DOES NOT DISCRIMINATE

Guilt has a way of piercing through even the toughest skin of mothers. It sees no boundaries geographic, cultural, age or otherwise and can often be found lurking in the undercurrents of arguments with partners, children and other family members. What's worse is that our kids are experts at knowing what to say and do to trigger feelings of guilt. The late Louise Hay said that guilt looks for punishment, and that punishment creates pain. She encourages us to forgive ourselves and others and to 'step out of your self-imposed prison'. Sound advice!

Where does this seed of guilt grow from? I believe it is so unique, this motherhood guilt, that it occupies its own little home within our bodies. For me, it is buried deep below my belly button. Starting as a deep-set churning in the gut, swirling and curling, it gradually pervades the entire abdomen region … then in swoops the fear—panic even—fuelled by the thoughts and imagined scenarios of all the possibilities of what could go wrong and incidents that could occur while I'm away …

I scrawled a line in my journal at the time of that plane trip that went something like *'I'm trying to make a sandwich without the bread'* and probably didn't realise how close I was to the truth. I opened my newly borrowed library book *'Mommy Guilt'*[1] to a random page and felt like the angel of motherhood had channelled herself directly onto it:

> *"We (mothers) give with little hesitation. Why, then, do we come to a screeching halt when we need to give to ourselves? Could it be that Mommy Guilt makes us believe that time spent on ourselves is time taken away from another family member? But, hey, aren't we also members of our families?"* (p181)

This final sentence stopped me dead in my tracks. *Yes, I am … aren't I? Where do my needs 'fit' in this newfound landscape of motherhood?*

This was so true and obvious and yet I realised I most certainly wasn't caring for my own self needs even at the most basic of levels. I think on the day I read this I had skipped breakfast and lunch and even given up on the cold cup of tea that sat paralysed in the microwave. I realised how much I had been beating myself up over my desire to take a break.

… That little voice in my head constantly jeering at me for needing alone time.

… That it was so selfish of me to want it, as if no other mother in the history of motherhood had ever needed a break to herself at this early demanding stage. The more hours of sleep lost, or the number of months or years passed without ever having a night off from their children was to be imprinted with pride on the skins of strong mothers who just put up with it.

… That my husband was the one who needed the break, not me.

What a load of bullshit was being fed into my mind, a smorgasbord of self-perpetuating doubt and diminishment! It needed to end!

Writing about it has helped heal my guilt. I want this book to be the catalyst that mows down these paradigms of guilt, fear, shame and worthlessness. I want you as the reader to hold this book and know you are worthy, entitled and deserving of your time out and your reconnection with the parts of yourself craving a resurrection.

I want you to know it is perfectly plausible for you as a mother to take some quality time out for yourself on a regular basis because *your needs matter as much as the rest of the family.*

I give you *permission* to make this happen.

Permission … to pause.

One word. Three syllables. Per-mis-sion.

Your tranquiliser for guilt and ticket to freedom.

PAUSE PROMPT
YOUR TANGIBLE GUILT-FREE PERMISSION NOTE

Something magical happens when we release ourselves from guilt and judgement. We allow ourselves space without feeling bad or unworthy about it. By taming our guilt, we can unblock the path to pockets of freedom in our days and lives. Use this book as your tangible permission slip to claim your own space as a mother and human being.

Carry it around with you in your handbag. You don't even have to read it! Just pull it out and hold it and know that it is there to support you and cheer you on. Show it to anyone who questions your desire for a break. Know that it has your back, and it believes in you on the days you feel like giving up. Guilt can paralyse us and prevent us from seeking opportunities for time out and space to ourselves. By recognising and facing the obstacles around guilt-ridden habits, we can open ourselves up to an improved sense of self-worth and confidence.

No matter what your situation, you are always deserving of a little space in your life.

Permission Note

I make peace with my guilt, so it can sit obediently by my side.
My guilt does not define me.

Chapter 3

Identity Hide And Seek

"It is frightening when a woman finally realises
that there is no answer to the question 'who am I?'
except the voice inside herself."

Betty Friedan

In a scene from the 2008 movie *'Marley & Me'*, Jennifer Aniston's character Jenny is completely wiped out by the demands of a newborn, toddler and a huge messy canine called Marley who is the central feature of the film. In one scene, Jenny's husband arrives home to find her fed up and exhausted, and they begin to bicker and argue. At the height of their argument, she exclaims how tired she is and that, 'I don't even know who I am anymore!'

I watched this scene just after my eldest daughter was born in late 2011. To my surprise, I was overcome with emotion and on the verge of tears. It was like gazing into a mirror pond. Whilst essentially a film about the life and antics of their family dog Marley, for me this movie was a reassuring hug from one new mother to another. Okay, okay, Jennifer

Aniston did not physically hug me, nor does she know me, but I hope you get my point!

I felt lost in my body and realised I simply had no idea who I was anymore. In the first few years of motherhood, I found it excruciatingly frustrating that my 'old self' had been stripped off so swiftly and abruptly that I completely forgot who I had been. 'Baby brain' may also have been a culprit to this, but there is much more to it. There is a whole book about it now, *'Baby Brain'*, published in 2023 by Dr Sarah McKay, but twelve years ago it was a misunderstood state of mind and often joked about side effect of pregnancy and early motherhood. I found myself reliant on the memory banks of family, friends and colleagues to recollect snippets of my career and education, freedom and independence.

'I cannot *wait* to get back to work when Kahlan is six months,' I proclaimed to my husband. 'Work will be so much easier than this.'

I longed for the nights when I sat freely in front of the heater with our dog Dexter and watched a whole uninterrupted episode of *'CSI'* or *'24'*. I yearned for the opportunity to procrastinate. I reminisced over being able to follow a train of thought from start to finish. I loved watching my daughter grow and glow with each new discovery, but at the same time I felt my own spark of discovery tapering away from me.

In hindsight, what I really lacked was support. I was adamant I could do it all on my own with ease and control. In reality, for most of the week, I was doing this parenting thing on my own. My husband left for work before 6.00 am and arrived home around 9.00 pm. He was, and still is, a hard worker, but he missed a lot of our first daughter's early life due to work commitments. We were both workaholics before becoming parents, however my work life encountered a swift and dramatic overhaul on the arrival of our first child. I had always been known for my job title or academic accomplishments. Now it was taken away from me, even if only temporarily. I felt lost, confused and alone in this new world of endless nappies, feeding, bathing and crying/settling. I felt so defeated and inexperienced.

> I scratched my head as to who I was, chasing an ideal of motherhood I now know just doesn't exist.

A journal entry from my diary at the time went something like this:

Last night I was up feeding at around 2.00 am, and I was awash with a feeling that our little addition to our family may not only be sucking milk from my body. She was sucking the absolute life and spirit from me to where I had no clue who I was or what day it was. I hope it gets easier the way every single person I bump into assures me it will.

Fast forward ten years on and I would love to say I've completely overcome the sense of self-sabotage, guilt, lack of self-worth and identity crisis. But this is untrue. I have learnt to *manage* my feelings around these concepts, but I am the first to admit they still have a habit of creeping in when I least expect. For example, in mid-2021, our youngest daughter was diagnosed with not one, but two rare eye conditions called *Orbital Cellulitis* and *Orbital Myositis*. The former is a bacterial infection of the eye socket that causes severe swelling around the eye. The eyelid swells so much it completely closes up, like a giant clamshell. It is a distressing sight to behold on a young child. Especially if it is your own child. *Orbital Cellulitis* can lead to sight loss and surgery in extreme cases. *Orbital Myositis* is an inflammation of the muscle near the eye that restricts eye movement and has been linked to a series of auto-immune diseases.

After being admitted to our local hospital, the severity of her condition increased dramatically, and we ended up at the Sydney Children's Hospital under the care and expertise of the country's top paediatric eye doctors. The most senior one admitted to having only seen a case like Avah's twice in his entire career. It was an emotional, stressful period, and I barely slept as I sat next to her in the hospital over the next few days. In the weeks that followed, I started to fall apart. This is a verbatim text I wrote to my husband at the time:

"I need to find ways of building myself up instead of beating myself down. I feel so worthless atm like I am failing at everything, especially at being a mum and a wife. I feel like I give so much of myself, but I just feel that overall, it doesn't seem to help the kids and their respect for me. I'm no fun anymore and I need to look after myself so much better after stressful periods like Avah's eye."

I have found that in motherhood we can become equal parts strong and vulnerable and that it is important to accept *all* parts of ourselves, else risk domination by the most suppressed of inner feelings.

PAUSE PROMPT
FIVE TIPS TO FREE YOURSELF FROM SELF-DOUBT

When we start to question who we are and what we stand for, we are also likely to experience episodes of self-doubt and sabotage. This has a sneaky way of shrinking us down to something we are not and talking ourselves out of all our positive traits. In my own experience, self-doubt, shame and identity-crisis have played out hand in hand. What follows is the personal five-step process I launch into action as soon as I smell a whiff of doubt creep in:

1. Immediately recognise the feeling
The first and most important action is to pause, close your eyes and accept the feeling of doubt that is arising. Attempting to suppress it or ignore it only gives it room to grow and morph. As you breathe in, imagine you are breathing in love. As you breathe out, imagine you are breathing out self-doubt. Place one hand on your heart and one hand on your belly

and repeat. Recognise you are not your self-doubt. Although you can welcome it to stay with you, it must obediently sit outside your body at your feet. It is not you.

2. Do *not* engage with the doubt in your own mind

Once you have consciously observed the doubt, breathed in self-love and allowed the doubt to sit outside of you at your feet, do not continue to encourage it in any way. It is now separate from you, and you have the power to keep it that way.

3. Do *not* reaffirm the doubt with other doubters

If there are people in your life, especially close friends or family members with a penchant for the 'glass half empty' way of life, do not in any instances contact them to talk about your issues with self-doubt. In my own experience, and you might relate, despite their best loving intentions these people in our life often inflame the feelings of doubt and self-sabotage and compound the effect rather than help it. Agreeing with you and affirming your lack of confidence in yourself only makes the situation worse.

4. Pick up the phone

Do pick up the phone immediately and call one of the positive lights in your life, the people that encourage you and always seem to offer the right advice no matter how bad you are feeling. For me, my first go-to is my best friend of thirty-five-plus years, Danielle, who always has a way of cheering me up and affirming all my good traits, even if none of them are shining bright on that particular day. She reminds me of who I am and where I have come from and quite frankly makes me laugh so hard that I almost wet myself! *This* is the type of person you want to talk to when you are down and out about yourself. Who is the Danielle in your life? Who is the person who has you rolling around in fits of laughter and smiling from ear to ear when you get off the phone? *Call them.*

5. Believe in yourself

This is the most important take away step. If you don't back yourself, how can others back you on your journey? We forget this so often as we tackle the tasks of motherhood and drown in our to-do lists. You are worthy. You are skilful. Your deep inner self is screaming at you to recognise this! Sometimes you have to let go of control, surrender to this mess of motherhood and let your inner spirit guide the way for you. Close your eyes, smile and know that you *are* love, and also loved.

Chapter 4

Domestic Drudgery:
Putting Space Before Dirty Dishes

"There's no need to try to be a superwoman...
A tidy house is a sign of a wasted mind."

Ita Buttrose

Cooking, cleaning, washing, ironing, vacuuming, mopping—how many hours a week do you estimate you spend on housework duties? It can become a thankless full-time load for an already busy parent trying to juggle the impossible demands of work-life 'balance'.

Every time I face the dreaded housework, my mind drifts back to footage of Jennifer Lawrence in 'American Hustle' playing a fed-up, strung-out mother. Relentlessly scrubbing away at a display cabinet with yellow gloves up to her elbows, she belts out the words to Guns n Roses' 'Live and Let Die'.

As she throws the vacuum cleaner from one side of her body to the other, singing and head-banging, her 'mum bun' falls apart and her hair becomes unruly. She continues to dance and crawl her way around the lounge-room while her little boy looks on unimpressed.

Leopard dress, murderous plot and sandals with
socks aside, there have been plenty of days
when I have related to Lawrence's character in
this scene.

I only have to watch it once to remind myself that I'm not alone in my blissless domestication.

A good friend of mine recently found herself working from home for three weeks. As a full-time working mum, her three kids were often in after-school care, with her getting home at around 6.00 pm each night.

At first, she was excited about spending so much time on the home front. But after the novelty of 'riding bikes to school with mum' wore off, she found herself feeling lonely, worn out and ready to get back to her workplace routine! The biggest impediment to her happiness during this time, she shared, was, '... *the fucking workload of meal preparation in a forever-hungry household, with dishes piling up and endless dirty washing … I feel like a slave in my own home, and I want to murder my husband.*' Despite her obvious plight, I found it refreshing to hear her recount this experience. The shock to her system. The ability to observe this situation from the perspective that many mothers have become numb to. It made me realise the domestic load on the home front is not normal. If we are the cohort of stay-at-home mums or mothers working from home, we should not discount the impact that endless thankless chores have on our daily lives.

My friend's story is also a reminder of the taxing toll the domestic load can have on the primary caregiver.

Not surprisingly, research conducted by the Australian Institute of Family Studies[2] reveals that mothers are still doing the 'lion's share' of housework, increasing from a weekly average of sixteen hours pre-children to twenty-five hours when they become a mother. Interestingly this statistic peaks at *thirty hours* when their youngest child starts school—the precise moment in time we finally reclaim back a little more space in our day! These findings are nothing short of appalling and one of the main reasons I have included this chapter in this book—to highlight the time chewed up by this benign pastime. It silently strips us of our space. And it needs to stop.

Motherhood metrics can be truly illuminating for our discussions on space and why it is so critical for mothers to get some. Use the metrics to help you formally justify your needs when explaining them to your family and co-caregivers. You know, the ones who need the science-backed evidence before they believe it can be a real thing—we all have them!

A 2019 survey of Singaporean mothers[3] revealed the plight that many modern mothers experience across the globe. Anger, frustration, anxiety and guilt were the top emotions listed that the majority of mothers identified with. *Three in four of the mothers surveyed agreed they do not have time for themselves,* and two in four admitted they rarely spend any time alone with their husbands. A key theme of the survey is 'Mothers need support and space for self-care'. I admit it's not a ground-breaking finding, but perhaps that is what is needed: more surveys that state the bleeding obvious and work up from there.

Over 17,000 mothers were surveyed in the 2022 State of Motherhood Survey, the largest statistically significant survey of its kind in the U.S. Sixty-seven per cent of mothers reported less than one hour of solo time per day that was not family or work oriented. A tiny eight per cent of mothers reported they receive the eight-hours sleep required each night for optimal human functioning. According to forty per cent of mothers surveyed, more help would make them feel more positive about their motherhood role. Ironically, plucking up the courage to ask for help is still one of the biggest impediments they face.

I often find myself contemplating the expectations on modern day mums and thinking it is no wonder we find ourselves feeling more anxious and overwhelmed than our pre-motherhood versions of ourselves.

The number one suggestion I make to other mothers is to avoid partaking in housework-related tasks when faced with a couple of hours grace to themselves. If possible, do the housework when the kids are in tow, or when your partner is around, even if it takes longer to complete. Believe me, I know this is no easy feat. It's tough to claim time out just for you when you have piles of washing loaded up, but your time alone is sacred and precious, *a rare jewel in the haystack of home life*. Unless you receive high levels of joy and uplift from scrubbing the floors or wiping mould from bathroom tiles, you may find yourself feeling deflated when you realise the lack of satisfaction this can cause.

When you do find yourself with a little stretch of space in front of you, that little chance to free yourself from the clutches of your children, try to avoid engaging in housework duties.

My biggest lightbulb moment on housework came when I found myself worked up and anxious before my husband arrived home from work one night. The girls were still quite young at the time, and I'd had an exhausting day of dealing with tantrums and outbursts, the stress of a project work and a baby that wouldn't sleep. By 6.00 pm, I still had no idea what we were having for dinner, so I threw together something in the hope it would come off as edible.

Leaving the kitchen a disaster area, I went to bath the kids and found myself in a near panic attack when I heard Glen get home earlier than usual. Despite all the challenges with the kids and work that day, I was gripped with anxiety that I hadn't cleaned up the kitchen like I normally did.

I now reflect on this and know it is completely acceptable, but in those early days of motherhood I still tried to project I was some kind of Super mum. I had clearly missed that memo. Add to that the guilt I felt that my working husband was coming home to face dirty dishes. But hold on a minute. Hadn't I been working too? Lastly, add in the now known fact that he didn't give a toss about whether the house was clean or not. He just wanted to see us after his day!

Letting go of expectations is the toughest process for a new mum. Swap dishes for a deeper connection with yourself and you will never look back!

PAUSE PROMPT
A SIMPLE MANTRA FOR OVERCOMING
DOMESTIC BLISSLESSNESS

Domestic duties have a way of sneaking in and stealing
our precious quality time. As soon as we clean up,
the kids mess everything up again. It's important to
temporarily disconnect ourselves from the ideal of
a perfectly spotless house, especially when we have
a rare moment to ourselves. If you find yourself at
home at lot, you probably relate a lot more to this
chapter than those away from the house. The chores
are staring you in the face multiple times a day.

Remember that old saying, *'out of sight, out of
mind'*? Use it as a simple but effective mantra for
cutting the cords that connect you to every daily
domestic job in your household. The dishes, the
washing, the vacuuming, the folding, the ironing, the
mopping, the wiping, the scrubbing, the soaking, the
packing, the unpacking and so on to what feels like
eternity!

Consider asking your partner or co-caregiver
if they can take on more of the load to help you out.
Do not feel guilt or shame in asking this, even if your
partner is the primary caregiver. A couple of domestic

chores off your list has the power to lift the veil off the relentlessness of household demands. You deserve to be free of some of these duties in equal measure. Alternatively, if your budget allows for it, consider enlisting the hired help of a cleaner, even if you only use them the one time. When my youngest was newborn and my eldest was a toddler, I unashamedly used a house cleaning service and arranged for the groceries to be delivered to my door. Although it was only once every two weeks for a few months, I could leave the house and domestics behind without guilt and know it would get done, eventually.

Permission Note

I leave the house, closing the door behind me, knowing that cleaning can always wait in the name of personal space.

Chapter 5

Resentment And Relationships

"Sometimes we need someone
To simply be there,
Not to fix anything
Or do anything in particular,
But just to let us feel
We are supported and cared about."

Day Writing Journals

My husband and I sat squirming on an uncomfortable sofa in a poky, windowless office. Bound together by blind faith, we felt like we were on trial for failure. After thirteen years of marriage, and twenty-two years in a relationship, we were marriage counselling virgins.

Until now.

His name was Joe, and his services came recommended by one of the relationships networks I had reached out to. Glen's only stipulation about the whole ordeal was that we saw a male, so here we were, with Joe. He might have been of Italian, or Greek heritage, I couldn't quite determine. As he rummaged around in the drawers of his English oak desk, he muttered to himself that he thought the forms were there *somewhere*. I glanced sideways at Glen, noticed an open crack in the white, worn wall, and used my eyes to trace it all the way up to the ceiling. I wondered whether it was deep enough for the roof to cave in on us. Or was that just wishful thinking?

He presented us with the 'forms' as if they were printed and embossed in pure gold, one for each of us. A survey for us to complete separately, right then and there. I found myself judging Joe already. This was our first appointment with him, our first appointment like this ever, and we were to silently survey ourselves? Had our marriage really been diminished to a set of multiple-choice questions, with scripted responses requiring zero space for personal original input? I stifled a giggle at the ridiculousness of the situation and proceeded with the task.

Ten minutes later, we both handed our completed forms in, ready for analysis. Joe 'ummed' and 'ahhed' at our responses, then asked us individually how we both felt. I think I replied with something like 'tired', 'stressed', 'sick of trying to be a perfect wife' or a mash up of all three of those responses. Glen might have gone with 'confused', 'overworked', 'just want life to be easy again'. Joe set us the task of organising a 'date night' for ourselves to have some alone time. Then the appointment was over, clipped promptly at the fifty-minute mark, with the promise of receiving our survey results via email within the coming days.

Our next appointment was locked in advance for a

fortnight later. On the morning it was booked, our eldest fell ill with an ear infection and couldn't go to school. Obviously, she couldn't come along to the counselling session with us either, so we tried to reschedule it. This proved more difficult and stressful than the counselling itself! I was shocked to receive frosty feedback from the marriage counsellor. We still had to pay in full for the service (around $250!) and the rescheduled appointment would incur the same cost. I'm sure the fine print listed all of this, but hey, when you are going for family counselling or marriage-related counselling, it is clearly the result of the pressure and impact of becoming new parents. Shouldn't there be some kind of empathy clause or understanding for last-minute cancellations of this kind?

Apparently not. It was laughable, so Glen and I laughed. It was nice to do that together, so we agreed we were done with marriage counselling!

From my experience, two key factors test your relationship like no other—long term travel and having children together. The latter is exacerbated further if you lack the support network of family or close friends. With no-one to alleviate the pressure in the early years and help pick up the pieces, it can be tougher to get your head around:

What the fuck you are meant to be doing, and;

When you get a break in this parenting gig?!

So, here's the truth. We did almost lose our marriage in 2018—around the time of the counselling session. Just when I thought we had cast that rollercoaster aside and dug deep into our pains and strains and learnt all our lessons, it threatened again in 2020. Sure, we hadn't planned for the stresses of COVID-19, and I don't know anyone who had: the home-schooling, the travel setbacks, the uncertainty and the living in each other's pockets thing. But I thought we coped quite well.

What I wasn't quite prepared for was how disconnected we became from each other in 2020 and how suddenly all the old wounds ripped open. Anger and resentment crept back in. It left me wondering how on earth this could possibly work? We seemed to have zero in common again. Glen was stressed with work, and I turned into a nagging mother and wife again, consumed by the cleanliness of the girls' rooms and the daily chores. My eldest was like a snowstorm every time she stepped foot into her room. I got so angry with picking up crap off her floor every day to no avail. I started to border on obsessive panic about the medication needs of my youngest if she hadn't had this dose by that time, and so on.

Eventually, my husband simply exploded at me, leaving me feeling raw and upset, confused and cranky. I felt like giving up on everything, including our marriage. I convinced myself I would be better off because I would finally get a break from being at the helm of the family. I cried for my late dog Dexter and my Pop and found I still had more to grieve for their recent losses. I cried over my recent estrangement from my dad that seemed to just happen like a poof of smoke. Two years had gone by without much of any word, and I calculated the kids and I had seen him only once in the flesh over that time, being Christmas Day 2019. I mourned for my fragmented family and my family home in the hometown I rarely visited.

I realised I still had some shit of my own to work through on a deep level. My inner child was still crying, and I needed to address that pronto.

And so, I ran away.

I'd had enough. I was scared about what I might do if I was pushed much further. I packed my bags and told Glen I was going away for a few days. I didn't know where, but the direction would be west. I still look back at this time with the prickle of a tear in my eye as I remember how worn out and strung out I was. I drove for hours and hours, tears streaming down my face, until I'd listened to enough Oprah podcasts and crappy radio channels to make myself laugh out loud.

I found myself in the outback town of Parkes in New South Wales, otherwise known for its huge satellite dish. They even had a movie made about it, appropriately named, 'The Dish'. And here, in this quaint little town, I made a friend by chance. Or was it? After pulling into the motel and unpacking my belongings, I cried some more, then pulled myself together to go get some takeout Chinese and a bottle of wine. I sat outside the door to my room, called Glen, told him I was okay, and that I'd be home in a day or so. This was not something I could have done if the girls were younger, so I do need to acknowledge how grateful I was for this—even if only in hindsight!

I closed my eyes and drew in a breath, opened them and immediately to my left was a lady with a glass of red wine smiling back at me. We cheers-ed each other, got talking and realised she too had run away for a night or two. What were the chances! We were right next door to each other! We talked and shared stories and laughed about how tough motherhood and relationships were. How much we loved our kids, but how desperately we needed time away from them every now and then. We drank (a lot) as she had a boot-full of grog that she'd brought with her from the pub she owned in Outback NSW. We laughed and cried together and were so appreciative of being able to openly share our respective stories with a virtual stranger.

I woke up the next morning nursing a sore head but with the motivation I needed to do some exploring and soul seeking. I didn't go too far, but I discovered some interesting local landmarks that reassured me someone was looking out for me that day. A cute little old church in a field of sunflowers with the most exquisite stained-glass windows was one such landmark. Parking my car and wandering around the building and property uplifted my spirits. I seemed to find an inner peace I hadn't felt for a long time.

> I let my guard down.
>
> I allowed myself to crack open and face the pain of the previous months.
>
> I felt lucky to be there, in that spiritual god-like field, without needing to worry about the welfare of my children.
>
> I suddenly felt a surge of gratitude for my husband, how good he was with the kids and how good we used to be together. Was I really willing to give it all up?

I acknowledged that I missed my little girls and Glen on a level so deep I felt an ache in the centre of my chest. And so, I pulled out my notebook and poured my heart out in the most illegible emotional scribble just to get it out.

What I realised at the sunflower surrounded church was that no-one was going to hand me a plate of space and demand I take time out for myself. It was *me* who needed to prioritise it. It was me who had to educate my husband and family that it was an essential part of my life now, and possibly the most important in improving my wellbeing.

PAUSE PROMPT
YOUR PARTNER, YOUR ENABLER

Asking for space or time out on your own takes courage and strength. No-one in your family is going to serve it up to you on a silver platter in the early days of motherhood. Often our partners don't even realise we need a break, and if they are the small percentage that *do*, they don't know *what* we need or *how* to help us get it!

Close your eyes and imagine you had no responsibilities other than your own desires and needs. What would you choose to do? Where would you choose to go? Write it down without feeling guilty for wanting it. And when the moment presents itself, approach your partner ... and tell them you need their support to make this happen for you. Whether it's a night off to catch up on sleep, a two-hour gym session, a long lunch with your girlfriends, an afternoon walk on the beach, a day to yourself in an empty house, a yoga retreat, an escape to a local winery, a cosy fireplace with a good book ... it's up to *you* to make it a reality! Your version of space will look different to mine, so use these as prompts only. Your innermost desires belong only to you.

Be bold and invite your partner or spouse to *enable* rather than *hinder* your pursuit of quality space for yourself. By working as a team together on it, they can understand your needs better and start to suggest their own ideas for your space-seeking quests.

If you are doing this parenting gig solo, the opportunities for claiming personal space will likely look different to those who have partners living under the same roof. How can you enlist the support of those closest to you (a parent, sibling, neighbour, colleague or friend) to help? Sometimes it is the people you least expect who are happy to help you the most. If you are co-parenting with an ex-partner, how can you use your time alone without the kids to light yourself up? What are you privately longing to do that is an impossibility with children at your ankles? Do *that* when you have your break.

Permission Note

My partner is my enabler to personal space and
growth as a mother. By inviting them in,
I can co-create a life of equality
and abundance.

Chapter 6

You Are Worthy Of Space

*"Free yourself from what others expect you to be,
and embrace who you are to the fullest extent.
That's beauty in its most pure form."*

Charlotte Freeman

I discovered the walking track by accident. Detouring deliberately off the main worn dirt trail, I opted for the route that led away from the signposted arrows. Ignoring the warning sign about steep inclines and unfenced cliff edges, I clamoured up the rocks and breathed in the fresh air and sweetness of solitude. Balancing my coffee cup in one hand, I pulled myself up and over the flat warm rock at the top.

Its heat was an elixir to my soul.

Standing tall, I made a conscious effort to connect with my newfound surroundings. The striking red and white native Christmas Bells were receiving a generous amount of attention by a swarm of bees, buzzing and sucking as they made their way from flower to flower. The soil was dark and damp, a consequence of the heavy rain from the night before. The fresh scent of eucalyptus filled my nostrils, and I wondered whether koalas were ever here, high in those treetops, munching away on the leaves. A pied currawong croaked in the distance, alerting me to its presence.

I sighed. What a morning. Not that it felt much different to any other. Yet the relentlessness of exhaustion had caught up with me, and I felt like I was running last in a most ungracious race. A race of resilience and regret for the parts of me I longed for. Would I ever entice them back, remember them as they were? Overcome this shame and unworthiness I felt so regularly these days? I dawdled slowly along the track, inviting my curiosity to befriend my uneasy sentiment. Was it sadness I felt? Disconnection? Dumbfounded-ness? All of that and more? Was I the only mother who felt she was swimming against the high tides of life, misunderstood and sick of explaining herself and her actions to those closest to her? How had I been stripped of my confidence, my spirit, my inner light that used to shine so brightly and joyfully? A bright yellow cluster of wattle caught my eye. *That used to be me*, I mused. *As bright as a sunflower in a full stretch of sun.*

Suddenly, the edge. I had already made it to the huge rock platform, a lid pressed down firmly atop the mountain. Freedom embraced every cell of my body. I forced out a smile and sat down cross-legged on the hard, warm surface.

A bee landed on my knee. Instead of brushing it off, I watched its yellow and black body move across my jeans until it reached a position of flight. Off it flew. How simple life can be if we just allow it to flow naturally, without force or obstruction.

In this short walk of fresh discoveries, I had saved myself. From myself. With a little help from a currawong, a wattle tree and a bee.

If you have flicked open to this page, or unexpectedly found yourself planted here like I did that day on the cliff face, you might be needing a little nudge of reassurance today to let you know how deserving and worthy you are.

PAUSE PROMPT
A LOVE NOTE

I have written here what I need to hear the most when I go through these deep, negative shit-talk sessions. I am giving you love through these pages and words, deep from the depths of my chest. Think of it as a little love letter, from one mother to another. Holding you if you feel you can't hold yourself today. Loving you if you feel it is impossible to find the courage to love yourself. And above all, reminding you of your worth and value to this world. This world that you have brought life into. This world where you have created sheer miracles by carrying and subsequently birthing a child into, enriching the energy of the planetary forces. You are strong, you are powerful beyond belief, and you are deserving of this time.

~

It might not feel like it,
but you truly are doing a great job
in the best way you know how to.
These times can be exhausting
and challenging to show up,
so please do not beat yourself up
for simply wanting a break.

You may be feeling misunderstood,
or irritated,
sad
or lost.

That is all perfectly
okay, my love.
Feel it,
but know that
you are stronger
and more powerful
than you will ever see
in this moment.

~

Permission Note

My worth is my gift to myself.
I see it, I know it and it cannot ever
be taken from me.

Chapter 7

A Sign And A Search Party

"All that is gold does not glitter,
Not all those who wander are lost;
The old that is strong does not wither,
Deep roots are not reached by the frost."

J. R. R. Tolkien, 'The Riddle of Strider'

I arrived at the two-day work conference dishevelled, tired and emotional. The little voice in my head reminded me I did not want to be here. Instead, I wanted (and desperately needed) a deep sweet sleep that lasted for days, wrapped warmly in the cosy comfort of my own company. I had been up all night, every night, for what felt like weeks on end, tending to the respiratory needs of my sick youngest child. A corporate work and wine junket was the last thing my nervous system could cope with.

On top of all this, somewhere in between the hospital visits and the meaningless endless meetings, I had come to realise I did not really belong in this 'old life' of mine anymore. I was drained of spirit and felt like an eel swimming against the East Australian current. My work did not excite me anymore. I was not connecting genuinely with my colleagues or clients. My passion was popped. Nothing and no-one made sense anymore. I seemed to spend half my time explaining and validating my ideas and decisions, making me even more tired than I already was.

Overnight bag in one hand and phone in the other, I arrived tardily at the Highlands guesthouse and took a deep deliberate breath. *You can do this, Teals.* My strategy mind clicked on, my game face woke up and I pushed forward into the foyer.

It was a cold afternoon, and the fireplace was crackling and warm. There were about fifteen of us, I guess, and we made our way to our lodgings to dump our stuff. My room was upstairs, a location I later lamented for its proximity to the reception desk.

First up was a session around the wine-tasting table, and the vino went straight to my head. Silently wishing I could excuse myself, we moved on to another tasting and then got ready for dinner and the evening session. I don't recall much of the meal or what we discussed, but afterwards we all gathered around the fireplace for some fun and light-hearted quiz games.

The flames were my friend. I watched them lick the wood and understood their message. I was toasted. And I wanted out of there. I needed to be alone in a desperate cardinal sense, and I could wait no longer.

At about 10.00 pm, feeling a little queasy, I silently excused myself, muttering something about needing to go to the loo and went outside instead. The briskness of the air literally took my breath away, but my nausea evaporated, and I slunk out into the dark night, free at last.

I found a small patch of grass right up in the back corner of the property. The night sky was dusted with a thousand stars, like half a cup of icing sugar sifted lovingly onto a pancake. It was magical, and I felt my muscles and abdomen relax for the first time in months. I pulled out my phone and popped on some tunes. *Man, I wish I had my jacket!* The temperature was two degrees Celsius, and I felt it deep in my exposed neckline. I didn't care. The peace and quiet was worth it.

The music stopped abruptly. A colleague was phoning, enquiring about my whereabouts.

'*Yep, I'm fine. I'm up in my room, really need the rest. See you in the morning.*'

Back to my subfreezing freedom and wonderful solitude. I contemplated my life as a mother, as a wife, as a worker. *Was there room to remember who I truly was in all this radical responsibility? Where was the time for me? And why was midnight on a work trip the only time available to process all this!*

Until this moment, I had forgotten what it felt like to tinker openly with my thoughts without distraction. It was like a reunion with a long-lost friend—me.

I had about five short minutes to relish it before I was swept back up into the chimney of conditioning.

A bright light flickered from the base of the hill. Then two. Three bobbing lights in unison hunted down their prey. I was the deer soon to be illuminated by the headlights of torches.

After the phone call from my colleague, she had requested the reception desk ring my room, only to discover I was not there. A search party ensued and my little gathering with myself was short-circuited. I remember stomping down the grassy incline of frost, filled with embarrassment, anger and shame. A lingering line from my brief and chilly interlude whispered to me in that moment. *You do not belong here anymore. Follow your heart and leave this old life behind. It is over.*

The following day was tough. I sat through session after session of strategic planning and brainstorming workshops, uninspired by any of the ideas shared. I watched the clock with such veracity that the ticking of its long hand became one with the pounding of my heart.

Driving home that afternoon, I gave myself permission to stop by the little creek at the end of our road before going home. I gazed into my reflection in the bubbling brook and committed to a pathway out of the only career I knew and one I had worked my butt off for over the past fifteen years. I committed to slowing down. I committed to starting again. All in the name of space and self-preservation.

This chapter of the book was not planned, and I might regret writing it, but it is one I felt compelled to share for any other mother feeling lost or stuck on her own career path. In my case, I let it get to a point of burnout where drastic measures were my only choice. Just to be clear I do not endorse solo drunken midnight escapades in freezing conditions! I pushed myself to fit back into my pre-motherhood work habits at the risk of my own health and wellbeing. I thought that by ignoring the smaller signs they would go away. Take it from me—they do not go, they only grow! I remember reading author Nikki Gemmell's story of her return to the workforce after having her first child. How she felt so reliant on her partner's income for the first time in their relationship, but how, despite her best efforts at trying, she just couldn't go back to her old workplace,

> "So I rang up my boss at the newsroom and it was great, because he was a father with young children as well, and I said 'I can't go back'. He said, 'Okay, you can go on a career break' and then I kept going on 'career breaks' for the next eighteen months and finally I resigned."
>
> Nikki Gemmell,
> 'Motherhood and Creativity: the divided heart'

My hope for this chapter is that you might prevent yourself from reaching the situation I found myself in at this work conference. I so desperately needed space to myself that I was willing to freeze under the midnight stars to get some sacred time between the cracks of dusk and dawn. There are easier ways. Identifying the clues and trigger points early on provides for a more planned and balanced approach to your career transitions!

PAUSE PROMPT
TRUSTING YOUR INSTINCTS

As mothers, each step we take after giving birth leaves its own unique imprint, creating a path of pressure marks as clues along our journey. The speed of the steps might be fast and furious, or slow and curious. They might move uphill or downhill, or trip and miss a step or two. They might drag and feel heavy or skip and feel light. Whichever way you walk your life in this new era of motherhood, know that it is the right path. If you feel something is no longer working, whether it be career or otherwise, trust your instincts, believe in yourself and follow your next step with your new sense of purpose. This can be scary as hell, but there is truly no better time to act than when the tides of the ocean of early motherhood are testing and caressing you. Because they are ultimately guiding you towards your burning passions and gut instincts about who you are and what needs to change in your life.

Permission Note

I am the only custodian of my passion
and purpose. I choose the path that
serves these best.

Chapter 8

Career Shifts Gear

"You did an MBA to run a yoga studio?"

Concerned family member

On 14 August 2015, at seventeen months old, my youngest daughter Avah took her first steps. It wasn't just a couple of steps, either. She pulled herself up to standing in the kitchen and tottered herself all the way across the tiles, before manoeuvring herself around the breakfast bar, and her older sister, until finally plopping her nappy-cushioned little butt down next to the lounge-room.

This was her 'first steps' milestone. She was a latecomer in the walking department, but she made up for it by taking twenty-seven steps at the one time.

Yep, twenty-seven!

I think I watched the footage my husband took of this moment about 900 times. I know the area of the kitchen she pulled herself up, the cute little pink pinafore she was wearing with matching leggings, the precise location she dodged Kahlan to prevent herself from getting knocked over, and the loud cheers coming from Glen who was recording her.

And I wasn't there.

I missed this precious moment because I was at work, trying to recover my career after two babies while my husband recovered from burnout due to overwork. Ahh, the irony! I'm happy to report in hindsight that we did finally achieve a more balanced lifestyle, but, at this moment in time, it was still many years away!

I didn't know this at the time, but about five weeks after her first steps, I would sit next to Avah's hospital bed, watching her struggle to breathe from pneumonia. This was the tipping point of the 'year that broke me'. My life was about to take some radical twists and turns, including my career.

The day after we got out of hospital, I made a number of commitments to myself that I felt would benefit my own health as well as the health of our family.

I announced to Glen that I would be commencing my yoga teacher training, and that I was going to be prioritising my non-business writing pursuits effective at the end of the year. I'd had it. I was done. And I've never been great at doing things in halves—I'm 100% in or not at all.

Every colleague, friend and family member could not make sense of this new direction. I had to dig my heels in very deep to follow it through. I felt so alone and out of my depth, but I also felt a strong primal instinct that I was definitely on the right path.

My gut agreed, so why shouldn't I?

I look back on this time as my toughest challenge yet. I'd

always readily taken advice and guidance (mainly from men, mind you!) on my studies, career and overall direction in life. Yet, something utterly carnal about the combined impact of motherhood, sleep deprivation and chronic stress tore at my heart and revealed my true self to the only person who could take action on my behalf—me.

I granted myself permission to pause and ponder the possibilities. And, once in sight, I sure as heck was not going to let them go.

One of my family member's immediate reactions to my decision was (verbatim), *'so you've done an MBA to run a yoga studio?'* This attested to why I hadn't plucked up the courage earlier in my life to follow the path that called me. And just to clarify, I was awarded a fully paid scholarship to complete my Master of Business Administration (MBA), so no one suffered any financial fee hardship on my part for my career pivot.

The disapproving response from those around me continued. One of my work colleagues spent a darn good part of her time one evening at work haranguing me about how I would never find another workplace that would provide the financial security I presently had. She shook her head like I was a silly little girl who had dropped her ice cream onto the pavement.

My husband despaired that in no way could we afford for me to do this, to which I proclaimed we could sell one of our lavish cars or, in the worst case, sell our house. It was so clear to me that our material possessions were controlling our lives a little too closely and we needed to flip this paradigm on its head.

Fuck it, I thought.

I'm just going to do it.

And I did.

And it worked.

Eight years later, it is still working.

PAUSE PROMPT
TWEAKING YOUR CAREER IS NOT A CRIME

You may or may not be in a position to make such radical changes to your own career in one sudden swoop. However, you may have noticed by now that work looks different after having children. It often takes a lot of juggling and trialling fresh ways of doing things before you feel any kind of balance. If this is where you are at right now, know that you are going to get there eventually. In your own way and in your own time, for the greater good of your own unique family composition.

Permission Note

I ponder possibilities without limitations
if my heart desires so.

Part 2

THE DISCOVERING

Chapter 9

When Fifteen Minutes
Is All You Have

*"We just need a moment,
or we're going to fall apart."*

Amanda King

I was on the phone with my sister in the car one night, and we were both talking on speaker without kids yelling in the background (a rare moment). It was a conversation that had been flowing without interruption or distraction and I wanted to hold on to it for longer. It was making me feel human and held, a sensation that one mother can only deliver to another.

We might have been complaining about our sleepless nights or the relentless nappy changes, the dinner making, bathing, feeding or the anxiety and guilt of leaving our kids at day-care. I can't even remember where I was driving home from as I'm rarely out after dark since having kids, but I recall with such clarity the moment I pulled into our driveway. I stopped myself short before saying to my sister that I had to go. At the same time, I thought, *do I? Couldn't I stay here in the car talking for a little longer?* I texted my husband (who was inside) and felt a wave of liberation.

Talking with Carls. Be inside in 10.

Why did I suddenly feel like a little kid alone in a lolly shop? Had my life become so 'spaceless' that I was *excited* to talk on a phone from the comfort of my *car* just so I could exist in my own company with the freedom of uninterrupted speech? The answer to this question was a resounding *'yes'*. I shared with my sister what I was doing and, low and behold, she was doing the exact same thing! We finished up the call ten minutes later, and I walked back into the house, uplifted and satisfied. This was all it had taken to turn my day around.

Years ago, I was chatting with an old work colleague who had two teenage children, and a husband working from home. On her workdays, she finished up at around 2.30 pm, but found herself resistant to going straight back to the home front. Instead, she started carving out a little quarter of an hour 'space wedge' for herself, dawdling in the streets lined with antique shops and allowing her mind and body to wander wherever it felt called to go. She did this three times a week, every week. It uplifted her spirits and enabled her to spend some time with herself at a soul level.

> *'The thought of going home to my husband and kids at that time of day made me feel a bit anxious, so I gave myself permission to stretch out my 'work' hours and give myself a break from the responsibility of it all. In that way, in those moments, I could just be me.'*

The best part about this story is that she kept this time all to herself. She didn't feel obligated to report about it at the dinner table on those nights. It was a secret shared with herself, and in a way, even more satisfying for the sheer *thrill* of it.

I'm so glad I took note of this conversation. It serves as a symbol in the life of a mother living in a busy household full of family members. She loves them all dearly, but she just needs a moment now and then to herself without feeling guilty for it. When she can't get that within the four walls of her home, she needs to think creatively about how she can access it from her routine outside of the home. It might be on the way home from work, like my colleague, or a stroll around the block before or after dinner—or any time that opens up to her in her day! Even if it means squeezing it in while waiting for children's activities to finish, such as my personal experience below.

My pre-planned fifteen minutes came on a Tuesday afternoon of no particular significance. The day so far had been a train wreck of appointments and tail chasing, notwithstanding the hour-round trip required to purchase a colourful assortment of party gifts, decorations and teeth-cracking candy for my youngest daughter's birthday party.

My girls and I were in the car after school pick-up, en route to swimming lessons. I was failing miserably at equally dividing my attention across each of their days' stories as they popped like table tennis balls from their mouths to my ears. I cared what they were saying, but I also needed silence. No sound. No movement. Just peace and quiet.

My attentiveness waned as I feigned an excited expression

for the benefit of the gaggling coming from the backseat. The truth was my mind was meandering in that calm but confident zone that can only be achieved when all members of the family are strapped into their car seats with the wheels in motion. No one can run off, there is limited scope for physical sibling in-fighting and the music or radio volume dial can be adjusted according to the tone and temperament of all passengers. What is it about driving in cars that grants our brain permission to slow down and think about anything other than the road ahead?

Back to the swimming route. Taking a deep inhale, I reminded myself of the spoonful of space I had to look forward to in my afternoon routine. A golden little window of fifteen minutes glimmering with hope and inner peace. It would occur during the overlap of my youngest and eldest girls' swimming lessons, specifically the quarter of an hour that sits nestled between 15:45 pm and 16:00 pm.

You might wonder what I did with this tiny slice of space in my day. The answer is simple.

Nothing.

I focused all my efforts on doing sweet fuck all.

And I did not feel one part guilty about it. Because I had *earned* it.

I resisted looking at my phone. I breathed in deep into my belly. I closed my eyes a crack, so it still appeared that I was watching my children swim—they regularly check on this during class! And I felt more centred and peaceful than if I had spent that time on a phone call or social media, or hurrying out an email.

You might think I am odd for placing so much value on a mere fifteen minutes of my day. Sometimes it does last longer, but on this Tuesday of no particular significance it saved my sanity. It nurtured my nervous system to resolve some knots of the day. It granted me with a permission note that was scheduled in my diary to pause and look after myself.

Afterwards, I could look at the night-time routine ahead with a renewed sense of optimism. I felt the distant thread of my innermost thoughts uncurling from a latent zone close to my base chakra. And I felt proud of myself for opening up a small slither of space, diligently and intentionally created, that would otherwise not have been within reach at all that day.

What I have learned and continue to learn is that a mother's space is not about bulldozing a valley into a monstrous mountain, or carefully and perfectly crafting the ideal week away or child-free overseas retreat. I believe as mothers, we don't need an expensive vacation or once-a-year weekend break—although they sure would be nice too! What we need is sacred moments of space in our day, *every day*, to lift us up and make us feel alive and free. Preferably solo and for at least fifteen minutes at a time. A meditation before school pick-up, a quiet hot cup of tea before bed, a breath in the breeze out on the back deck, a careful tending to our favourite flora friend in the garden.

PAUSE PROMPT
MAKING YOUR FIFTEEN MINUTES COUNT

If you have the chance for as little as fifteen minutes completely to yourself on any given day, what could you do to replenish yourself? Could you:

- Lie on your back and elevate your legs up the wall, instantly improving your circulation and mood?

- Put your phone out of reach for fifteen minutes, sit outside in a comfy chair and close your eyes?

- Drive the long way home if you've been out or working, preferably with an outlook of nature and a speed zone slower than eighty km/hr?

- Walk or ride your bike around the block?

- Pick some fresh flowers from your own garden or park?

- Dedicate fifteen minutes to writing out your feelings in your journal, or drawing or doodling whatever comes into your head, old style, without seeking out your device?

- Enjoy a sweet cup of tea or coffee and make it the only thing you do for those fifteen minutes?

- Read a chapter of that book you've been meaning to start on?

Permission Note

I can make fifteen minutes feel like an hour
if I slow down each and every second of
every minute.

Chapter 10

Disconnect To Reconnect

"Almost everything will work if you unplug it
for a few minutes, including you."

Anne Lamott

Slowly depressing the brake pedal of my car, I pulled into the closest carpark at the beach headland. The vastness of the ocean had an immediate calming effect on my overactive mind, and I paused to take in this moment. I had been planning this all day and was proud of myself for getting here. I had a whole thirty minutes before school pick-up, and I was going to use every miniscule minute to my advantage.

I wound down my car window, closed my eyes and inhaled the salty air deep into my lungs. Like an instant purification, it was the internal cleanse I had been longing for in my day of irritations and chores.

Aaaaaand … release.

Breathing out, I gazed out at the green grassy headland and watched a young family exploring the edges as if for the first time. Donning matching jackets and gloves, with windswept hair tamed by holidaymaker hats, the family of four looked out at the crashing waves as the young siblings squealed with delight. The mother reached for something in her bag and called the other family members over. It was selfie time. They cuddled in together as she angled the phone towards the sky with the camera facing towards them. One take, two takes, three … nope, the lighting or angle must be off. Or it might have been a shocker of the mother, in which case she will keep going until it fits the ideal 'look' she's going for on Instagram. Harsh, but we all know it's true!

Shuffling sideways like a mud crab, the family stuck together in formation and attempted another happy snap. Still not the goods. *Just one more,* I could make out the mother saying to her partner and kids. In her head she would be wondering whether this last one could be a keeper for the 'gram. Add in a 'gingham' filter and it might just scrape through.

The holidaymaker kids looked relieved to resume cartwheeling with freedom across the grassy knob of the headland, only to be ushered back to the car by their parents. The picture had been taken, and now onto the next landscape …

Are our lives destined to be controlled by palm-sized, attention-seeking, demanding little devices?

Johann Hari wrote a brilliant book called '*Stolen Focus*', published in 2022, that explains why our attention spans have been diminishing for decades, and the role technology has played in accelerating this worrying trend. He questions what we can do to reclaim our focus and ultimately live meaningful lives, highlighting the importance of flow state and play for today's children. The freer play a child receives, the more solid a foundation they will have for their focus and attention. As adults, our flow state is also an important facet in our ability to focus.

> *"I noticed that if I spent a day where I experienced three hours of flow early on, for the rest of the day, I felt relaxed and open and able to engage – to walk along the beach, or start chatting to people, or read a book, without feeling cramped, or irritable, or phone-hungry. It was like the flow was relaxing my body and opening my mind... I felt myself falling into a different rhythm.*
>
> *I realised then that to recover from our loss of attention, it is not enough to strip out our distractions... We need to strip out our distractions and to replace them with sources of flow... we all have a choice now between two profound forces – fragmentation, or flow. Fragmentation makes you smaller, shallower, angrier. Flow makes you bigger, deeper, calmer. Fragmentation shrinks us. Flow expands us."*
>
> (Hari, 2022, p56-8)

In an interview in 2001 with Apple cofounder and billionaire Steve Jobs, he told *Newsweek* he would trade all his technology to spend an afternoon with Socrates.

Let's stop and think about this for a moment.

Why would the actual *creator* of our smartphone devices desire the opportunity to trade all his life's work just to sit with a Greek philosopher? It's an interesting (and haunting) question to ponder. One you might find the answer to once you take some time out from your device yourself. In his book, Johann Hari echoes the sentiments of Steve Jobs by sharing a story from a speech by former Google strategist, James Williams. In addressing an audience of hundreds of leading tech designers, Williams posed a question to them.

"How many of you want to live in the world you are designing?"

It was met by silence. Not one of the Google tech leaders raised their hand.

Sometimes, especially as busy mothers, we need to truly disconnect from technology in order to reconnect with our inner voice and sacred centre. Some of us are lucky to remember a world without smartphones (or even internet!). If this is you, close your eyes and take yourself back. For me, I imagine myself at ten years old in 1991, swinging on the vines in the bush at the back of our home. Creating a 'swing box' out of an empty cardboard beer box with my sisters and friends for our dog Tex to be pushed in. Digging clay from the backyard to make bowls and plates for a tea party. Swimming in my friend Haley's murky dam on her family's property in Bergalia. Roller-skating on the cement slab that would become the floor of their new family home. Horse riding.

I invite you to work with me on this concept with an open mind. This chapter is not about dissing our devices and never using them again. It's about taking back control instead of jumping to attention at every notification, 'ping' of a text message or late-night work email demanding an immediate response.

In an article I wrote in 2016[4], I researched the impacts our smartphones were having on our lives. Some of the statistics and findings left me with a deep sense of sadness and lament. A survey from the United Kingdom revealed that smartphone users check their devices an average number of 221 times each day! A town in Bavaria installed traffic lights on the ground to prevent pedestrians from walking into oncoming traffic. China created 'texting lanes' on footpaths for people who preferred to walk with their head stuck in their device.

Am I the only one who thinks this is all levels of wrong?

Psychologist Marny Lishman[5] reported that therapists are finding it hard to keep up with the increasing levels of social media addiction. She says that people are not getting enough time in the day to simply do nothing.

"We are filling blank moments that your body would normally be recharging, and the minute you read social media your brain is firing, it's making judgements, it's stressing."

I had no idea how to control my smartphone affliction until I consciously created space in my life to exist without the constant demands and naggings of my iPhone. Looking back, I recall the exact night I decided to disconnect more regularly. I had taken myself to bed at 10.00 pm to get an early night before work the next day, but as I dropped my head to the pillow, I heard my phone vibrate next to me on the bedside table. Next thing I knew it was two hours later, and I had written a post through the Facebook app, scrolled Instagram and Twitter, and written four emails back to clients. It was a case of 'enough is enough'. I genuinely felt like my device was controlling me and not the other way around. To top it off, I was absolutely exhausted.

> Smartphone, tablet, laptop or desktop, don't we owe it to ourselves to stop and just be? To think for ourselves, even if just for a walk around the block?

If we calculate the hours spent each day trawling through our smartphones, imagine how much precious time we could have to ourselves?

PAUSE PROMPT
SIX TIPS TO DEVICE FREEDOM

After trialling a few ideas and observing how I felt before and after, I came up with a list of six tips to support me in seeking out 'phone-free time', even if it was just for an hour here or there. It wasn't a case of vanquishing my device forever. It was about being proactive and empowering myself to become the boss of my own time. Use these tips for inspiration or create your own list of phone freedoms.

1. Leaving my phone in the kitchen before going to bed. This was tough at the start once I realised how much I relied on my phone in a multifaceted sense. It's a torch to light the way to the bathroom or kids' room during the night, an alarm to wake me up of a morning or a crutch to default to if I need 'connection' when I first wake up. But this one decision has been truly liberating and helped me regain a sense of control over a device that controlled my every move. It doesn't have to be the kitchen, just anywhere out of reach that you can't extend your arm and latch onto it. I have been doing this now for seven years and I can't imagine sleeping with it next to me anymore.

2. Walking (the dog) without my device. This is a really simple exercise—and can be implemented minus the dog if you don't have one! Try it and see how free you feel, even if just for half an hour.

3. Reading a book. A real, tangible, paper-feel book. One you can earmark or scribble notes in. Whatever takes your fancy. Try it. It is almost ethereal when you read an entire chapter without being able to click to another page via a hyperlink.

4. Visiting the local gardens or a natural open space. There's something about our natural landscapes that slows us down and reverses the urgency of the world. A short break to a park, beach or bushland has the power to retune our heart strings and return us to our natural cellular state of being. Even a stroll in your own backyard can work miracles. Take a moment to listen to the birds. Smell the flowers. Perch yourself on a tree branch. It is amazing how much detail we miss when we're glued to our screens.

5. Attending a yoga class. Or any class that requires your device to be buried deep within your belongings. Leave your shoes at the door and stretch out for an hour in device-less bliss. Sit with yourself in meditation and breathe in the benefits.

6. Turning off notifications. This one was an absolute game-changer for me. Consider turning your phone to silent and turning off as many notifications from as many apps as possible. This helps limit the reactive responses to comments, texts and calls and gives you back control of your device in a proactive way. If you expect to receive calls that require your immediate attention, keep it off silent but try to only respond to calls and nothing else. Make best friends with the

'Do Not Disturb' feature in your phone settings and consider scheduling it to come on at the same time each night.

Other experiments I have trialled include undertaking a 'digital detox' from time to time to cleanse myself of my social media habits. In 2020, I lasted twelve days off social media[6] and removed around twenty apps from my iPhone. The effect was immediate—I felt instantly lighter, clearer and empowered. I was in the driver's seat of my own device, and it made all the difference to my phone use and mental health.

You are going to get through this, even if it is with a little help from an indoor playcentre that serves up coffee and warm smiles.

Permission Note

I value my device-free time as if it is the most sacred time of my day.

Chapter 11

A Hot Cup Of Tea
— Is It Really That Hard?

"I distinctly remember sitting exhausted in our little work cottage in Wales and thinking that I would fucking pay someone to come over and just make me a cup of tea."

Lily Mae Martin

When I look back on my childhood, I have a strong memory of my parents sitting on the front step of our family home in the small coastal town of Tuross Head. They often sat for hours on a Saturday morning in the sun, drinking cups of tea or coffee and reading the ultra-sized Weekend version of The Sydney Morning Herald. Back in those days, cafes and coffee shops weren't a thing yet, especially not in smaller villages. If you made your coffee using Moccona from a fancy glass jar, you were considered a coffee expert.

My sisters and I had the task of 'making' the coffee for Mum and Dad. We were too young to boil the old-fashioned iron kettle from the gas stovetop, so we were instructed to use the microwave. Whoever's turn it was would be so excited to take on this important job and deliver each freshly microwaved cup with pride and purpose.

I attribute this ritual from early in my life to my adult-life appreciation of the value of a hot cup of tea. Like a family heirloom, it has been carefully passed down. But I took most of it for granted. I was ignorant to this simple practice of sitting in peace, sip by sip, *until* I had children myself and they were way too young to be microwaving tea for me. I could have lavishly indulged in as many cups of tea as I desired, appreciating each connection between my mouth and the lip of the cup, at many points in my life before I had children. My freedom frolicking around me in a swarm of under-appreciation, secretly cackling as it foresaw my future through its prophetic lens. It knew—it *knew* once my inaugural egg of conception was released from my fresh young ovaries into my fallopian tubes that it was only a matter of time before I repented my earlier ignorance.

When was the last time you sat for ten whole minutes focused on nothing but your hot cup of tea or coffee?

Let me introduce Anne. She knows the value of her morning cuppa.

Anne and I met at Wednesday morning swimming lessons in about 2018. We would often sit together and have a chat whilst our girls were in the pool. She was going through a tough time on the home front, including a breakdown with her partner, and was facing the imminent role of single parenting.

I admired her for her courage and conviction to stay true to herself no matter what and enjoyed our weekly chats. What I remember most about her, though, was a comment she made in passing one week about her mandatory jumbo takeaway coffee, which she always purchased just before the class.

> 'I don't know what I would do without this cup each morning. For me, it's the liquid equivalent of a hug.'

That comment stuck with me because it held so much truth. It says so much about what we crave as parents. Comfort. Support. Empathy. Connection. What is it about a hot cup of liquid that uplifts our morning, afternoon or evening? I recently read of a scientific study in the United States[7] that found holding a cup of hot coffee could make you feel friendlier to someone you have just met, compared to holding a cup of iced coffee. Is it the warmth that we crave? Associated with safety and comfort, this may be true. Researchers also suggest that the warm sensations activate a part of the brain where judgements occur, making us less critical and judgemental of others.

THE 'COFFEE COMPASS'

What can we tell about our own state of mind from our 'drinking habits' (of the warm, caffeinated variety)? For mothers, our daily cup of tea or coffee can reveal a lot about how we feel and how we're coping at that moment.

If we have microwaved our cup more than five times to keep it hot, it can be a clear indicator we haven't managed to carve out any time for ourselves that day—and we probably feel it. In a way, our coffee or tea drinking habits act like a barometer or a compass, pointing out the quality of our day and our emotional wellbeing.

I know if I can start my day right with some yoga and mantra meditation, followed by a fresh, hot coffee made with loving intention, I feel on top of the world and ready for anything. On the contrary, if I sleep in, feel sluggish and forgetful, argue with the kids before school and get behind on my project work, I feel like I'm chasing my tail all day and it impacts my spirit. Despite all my spiritual training, I am not immune to a desperate coffee run via a Macca's Drive Thru! I can transform from a calm yogi into a psycho, stressed-out mama in no time if I cannot get the space and quiet time I need.

Can you relate to days like these?

Having someone come and hold my baby for me or make me a cup of tea or coffee was right up there in my list of 'wins' in my first year of motherhood.

'TEA CHAN'—A TEA MEDITATION

In 2015, as part of a silent meditation experience at my local Buddhist temple, our group of fifty (who were not allowed to speak to each other for the duration of the retreat) were introduced to the fascinating practice of 'tea chan'. The term 'chan' comes from the Sanskrit word '*dhyana*' (meaning 'meditation' or 'meditative state') and 'tea chan' involves an ancient tea ceremony that encompasses the use of sight, sound, taste and observation of inner thoughts, similar to the state of meditation. According to Venerable Master Hsing Yun[8], just as sitting meditation leads to 'chan mind', so too does this tea ceremony.

Offering four principles, including harmony, reverence, purity and tranquillity, tea chan practice promotes harmony between people and nature, and purifies the inner self. It is believed that the purity and nature of the tea is a spiritual experience, considered a 'spiritual refreshment'. I thought that was pretty cool.

This traditional practice reveals what mothers everywhere seem to have known for generations—that a hot cup of tea can hold a special space for us. It offers ten exclusive minutes of peace and warmth, and a connection to ourselves that goes much farther than skin deep. It is a delicate thread of a larger and more exquisite layer of life that reminds us of our important place in the world.

PAUSE PROMPT
HOW TO GIVE 'TEA TIME' MORE MEANING

As mothers and caregivers, is it possible for us to create a little wedge in our day dedicated to our hot drinks? Here are a few pointers to get you started:

1. If there is somewhere in your house, like a balcony or front yard that offers a nice sunny sitting position, or while on your morning walk, take the time to stop and

sit for a length of around ten minutes if possible. I aim to sit in peace with my coffee after my morning yoga and before my kids get up. It's not always possible, but the perfect time for me is around 6.30 am. The birds are up, but the neighbourhood is quiet. The lawn mowers are yet to kick in and the rush of the day is still an hour or so away. When my youngest was still at the age where she fell asleep on a pram walk, I picked out the brightest, sunniest looking long wooden chair on our morning walk in the gardens or at the beach. This was the time I ensured I took my first sip (usually as soon as her little eyes closed from the movement and gentle rocking of the pram). Choose your time and your perch and make it special. Planning is required to get the timing right, so make sure it moves in the flow of your day, not anyone else's.

2. Slow it right down by activating your senses. If it is not possible to sit and appreciate your cup in peace, you can still slow the process down by shifting your awareness to your sense of smell or touch. Breathe in the strong scent of the beans or leaves before you take your first sip. Close your eyes, even if for just a moment. Focus on nothing but the first sensation of heat on your lips. Appreciate the moment, take it slow and introduce this new practice into your daily 'grind'.

3. Before bed ritual. If you feel you have no time during daylight hours to stop and sip slowly, consider the space right at the end of your day. Oftentimes, when I have had a big day with no break and I couldn't even tell you what I ate for lunch let alone what time I gulped down my tea or coffee, I take myself to bed as early as possible, cradling my chamomile tea and candle like my life depends on it. I dim the lights and sit on my mat or the carpet at the end of my bed and place my rose quartz candle out in front, aligned with my body. Sitting cross-legged or kneeling (a chair is another option), I close my eyes, breathe nice and deep into my abdomen and hold my hot cup of herbal tea and honey up to my mouth. I take a slow and deliberate sip and continue until complete. I always notice how much calmer I am as I hop under the sheets with a warm belly, ready for anything the night might bring. I feel better prepared for the waking, teething, feeding, bed-wetting and nightmares if I've taken the time to sit with my cuppa before bed.

Chapter 12

A Crack In The Calendar

"She stood in the storm,
and when the wind
did not blow her way
she adjusted her sails."

Elizabeth Edwards

On a bright, sunny afternoon in early 2017, I was looking forward to celebrating the birthdays of two of my girlfriends at one of the local bars at Wollongong's North Beach. The plan was to have cocktails and drinks, followed by dinner and more drinks. My pre-motherhood self was having a little party of excitement inside my belly at the prospect of unwinding, giggling, dancing and letting loose from the demands of the household, but my post-motherhood self was looking back to the last time I let my hair down with my girlfriends. Recovery the day after and feeling like shit for a week.

I decided to commit to using this break from the house for socialising *and* spiritual time. To ensure this would be possible and to stay strong amidst the frivolity, I drove my car to the party. It was in an area I didn't want to leave it overnight, so I was sure I wouldn't be talked out of driving home.

It was the best night. I had a couple of drinks and loads of laughs with my girlfriends, followed by glasses of water and an early exit before it got too dark. I remember the surprised looks on my friends' faces when I excused myself from the party in the name of meditation! This very moment was the secret ingredient to succeeding in my intentions to create sacred personal space in fresh and creative ways—and the opportunity to move past the judgement of others and truly let go of what they might think of me. In my experience, my friends and family have ultimately respected me for my newfound ideas. Well, maybe not at first, but they eventually got used to it.

I knew if I reached my special rock at the beach before sunset, I could slow myself down and meditate before going home. Yep, I left the party so I could meditate! My younger self would not understand, but I didn't need her to. This was me now, prioritising my health and space, and I liked this version of myself a lot better.

As I parked my car and made my way to my meditation rock, a huge smile spread across my face. I felt empowered and strong, courageous and calm. I had created a quiet contemplative space for myself off a crack in the calendar. It was possible. And I would continue to find creative ways of carving out my 'me time' by prioritising what was best for me, not others.

Repeat after me:

This is not selfish.

This is essential.

PAUSE PROMPT
CALENDAR HACK

Seeing it all on one page or screen, take a good look at your monthly calendar. Whether it is on your phone, or a hard copy version hung up in the kitchen like mine, make sure it's the one that includes every family member's activities, appointments, events and deadlines. It's usually the one that you, the mother, works her day from. Why look at a monthly schedule and not a weekly schedule? Simple. Because I'm inviting you to consider realistic opportunities for personal space. If you look only at the next week, it will probably depress you into giving up!

Try not to find a completely free day—although if you can reserve that to yourself definitely do it! Instead, see if you can find an appointment or event already listed on a particular day. It might be a doctor's appointment, a swimming carnival, a work meeting or a parent teacher interview. Make sure it is something you are required to be at. Place a red asterisk before or after your chosen calendar item. This asterisk is your 'calendar crack'. You can name it if you like, for example, 'mummy's appointment', or just keep it as an asterisk, so only you know what it's for. Just like my meditation session at the beach after attending my friends' birthday party, it can become a private appointment with yourself to look forward to.

Now that it's included in your calendar, you are making a commitment to yourself to reserve thirty to sixty minutes of precious personal space just for you. By looking for little windows of opportunity when you are trapped by the demanding schedules of everyone else in the family, wondering if you are ever going to squeeze your needs in, you can feel empowered and free by reserving this time. It might not seem like much, but if you are new to this 'space creation' idea, it is a great springboard to becoming more and more confident at claiming the time you need without feeling guilty or unworthy.

A monthly outlook shows up to thirty-one days, including four or five weekends. I find this is the perfect number to step back and see the opportunities for our own little time slots of space to emerge.

A little loophole here and there can weave wonders into your day, week and month. And the best thing I've learned? No-one else in your family needs to know about them!

Permission Note

When I actively choose to look at my busy
schedule with a fresh set of eyes, I discover
small slithers of open space just for me.

Chapter 13

Breathing Space

*"A yogi measures the span of life by the number of
breaths, not the number of years."*

Swami Sivananda

An intuitive acupuncturist once told me that no matter what,
my breath was always there to support me and no-one could
take it from me. A quiet round of breathing with eyes closed,
following the breath down deep into my belly, could work
wonders, even if just for a few moments.

This advice took on new meaning a few short months
after it was shared with me.

It was July 2015 and, unbeknownst to me, my system was
about to shut down on itself. I think it was sick of sending
signals that were being blatantly ignored and refuted. It
needed to do something high impact to wake me up from
my ignorance. I had been told by a number of doctors that I
needed to start taking my health seriously, that my ill-health
was predominantly stress-induced and lowering these stress
levels would result in a happier body and mind.

I have always been strong-minded (and probably a tad stubborn too!) and thought stress was too 'fluffy' a notion to be causing it all. In the business world I worked in, stress was always seen as an essential part of life. In fact, I thought I recalled a saying once that some stress was even 'good' for you? In any case, I was too busy with work, a baby, a toddler and a burnt-out husband to have time to focus on my own health issues. Looking back, I see how obvious it was, but at the time I needed a real curveball to knock me off my feet and force me to take notice.

Tick!

It was a Thursday evening and I was still at work, despite a gradual sensation of nausea developing throughout the day. My work colleague, Alex, and I were the only ones left in the office. I looked over at her and shared how unwell I was feeling, and she encouraged me to head home immediately. I packed up and drove home to find my baby asleep and my eldest child, who was three at the time, in the bath. My nausea had increased significantly during the drive, and I took myself to the kitchen where I started to breathe quickly and heavily.

I placed my hand against the kitchen wall to steady myself. I wasn't sure whether I was about to vomit or pass out. Then, I felt a sensation in my stomach like no other I have ever experienced in my life. The best description I can give is that the muscles inside my stomach and abdomen region felt like they were inverting to turn inside out. My ten fingers curled in dramatically, but not in synchronicity. They were stuck halfway between an extended position and a fist pump. I yelled out to my husband Glen who ran in and saw me, caught me before I collapsed, and carried me to our bedroom whilst willing me to breathe.

'Call an ambulance,' I said to him between gritted teeth and a locked jaw.

By this stage, I could barely move my mouth or invoke any kind of expression. It was like rigor mortis of the face.

I recall Glen screaming down the phone, saying my face and lips had gone blue. Out of the corner of my eye I saw a little shadow pass by the doorway. Her tiny silhouette in our bedroom doorway and her big frightened blue eyes still haunt me. It was, of course, my three-year-old daughter. I often pray this is not a memory she will recall as one of her first when she is older.

I have no recollection of the five minutes that followed, but there was a flurry of activity once the ambulance pulled into our driveway and the paramedics (one male and one female) rushed into our bedroom. They started doing tests and observations as my heart rate finally eased up. Someone placed a plastic bag over my mouth and told me to continue breathing slowly into it if I could. The nausea crept back into my stomach as it started to untwist and release.

I felt enormous waves of emotion and gratitude towards the strangers sitting on my bed, bringing breath back into my lungs.

'You have experienced a very severe type of hyperventilation,' the woman said. 'You should have passed out, but your husband held you up.'

Hyperventilation? It didn't sound serious enough for what just happened to me. I was mentally strong and capable, so why did this happen to me? I double-checked with the female paramedic that I wasn't going to die.

'No,' she responded. 'But you are going to have to make some very important decisions about your health and lifestyle to prevent it from happening again.'

'Some mothers have a little glass of wine at the end of their day to ease their stress,' her male counterpart chimed in.

Could the cure for this harrowing experience really be a plastic bag over my face paired with a crisp tumbler of vino?

I was baffled by this diagnosis and shocked that my body could contort into such shapes beyond my control. But it was the restriction of my breath for those precious minutes that scared me the most. *What if it happened again? What if I was driving with my girls in the car? How would I ever forgive myself if something happened?* After I was able to breathe again, I vomited for twelve hours straight. It was like a physical and psychological cleansing pivoting me away from stress, trauma and burnout. I had in recent months been diagnosed with a type of thyroid disease called *Hashimoto's Disease*, an autoimmune condition that treats the thyroid as a foreign object, subsequently seeking to destroy it. Was this newly diagnosed condition of mine somehow responsible for this terrifying incident?

Those paramedics were my angel guides that night. My brush with breathlessness became an essential cog in the wheel of motion towards claiming my space as a mother. A short time later, I enrolled in the yoga teacher training course I had been daydreaming about for years and with the guidance of my teacher trainer, Simon Borg-Olivier, I relearned how to breathe. In the years to come, I would start to teach others about this transformational technique. You can try out a simple version for yourself below.

PAUSE PROMPT
A SIMPLE FIVE-MINUTE BREATHING EXERCISE

Find a quiet area where you know you won't be disturbed for at least five to ten minutes. Just before you hop into bed for the night is a perfect time for this, or any time you might be feeling overwhelmed or anxious. Lie on your back with a blanket over your body (optional).

- Allow your entire body to sink into the floor, carpet, mat or whatever surface you are on. On a warm sunny day, you could even lie out on the grass and sink into the earth.
- Let your feet fall away from each other and feel your calf muscles spread out and relax. Place your hands palms up for receiving or palms down for grounding.
- Close your eyes and let your eyeballs roll back into their sockets, nice and heavy.

- Take a deep long breath in through your nose, keeping your mouth closed if possible, and inhale deep into your abdomen area. Relax your tummy like a baby and allow it to pop out as you breathe in.
- Let the air come out on its own after you reach the top of your breath—the length of each breath varies from person to person. As you release your breath, feel your body becoming heavier.
- Sink deeper into your floor, mat, ground or whatever surface you are on.
- Keeping your eyes closed, place one hand on your heart and the other on your tummy.
- Take a second deep breath in through your nose and feel the air as it enters each nostril. Feel your lower hand as it is gently pushed away by your tummy. This is how you know if your breath is in the correct place—the lower hand rises and falls as you inhale and release each breath.
- Continue as many rounds as you like, reconnecting with your breath and allowing your body to sink deep and open up space within.
- *Optional:* Position your legs up a wall, keeping your sitting bones slightly away from the wall. Relax the legs, allowing the knees to bend slightly and feet to fall away from each other. Repeat the steps above with your legs in the new position.

Permission Note

Breathing deeply and slowly into my belly frees
me from the anxieties of my day.

✦

Chapter 14

Desperate Days

"Your now is not your forever."

John Green

Another day ricocheted off the last. I had no idea which one it was, only that it was day instead of night! I paused and reflected on my state of being. I felt low, unmotivated and devoid of disposition. But I didn't have time to worry about it. Avah, a baby at the time, was screaming for a feed and Kahlan, my toddler, was climbing the toilet step to practice her number twos. They jolted me out of my momentary melancholy.

Latching Avah to my breast, she started to feed at the same time as Kahlan declared faecal success from the bathroom and her need for me to *'wipe my bum, mummy!'*. Still breastfeeding, I stood up and held Avah in 'football hold' with my left arm, with her head secure in the palm of my hand. I positioned her firmly against my chest and under my arm as I used my other hand to tear off some toilet paper and help Kahlan wipe her bottom.

I declared out loud that we were heading out this morning to *Green Bean*. This was the only place I knew where I could sit with a cup of coffee, my sleeping baby in her pram by my side, and let my rambunctious three-year-old run safely and freely without needing to intervene.

Ahh, *Green Bean*. An oasis for sleep-deprived, coffee-desperate, malnourished young mothers yearning for a moment's reprieve. An indoor space with a jumping castle, slippery dip, cubby houses, dress ups and age-appropriate music. I was prepared to organise my entire day around a visit to this place, just to get fifteen minutes of pause.

Stuffing the nappy bag full of wipes, nappies, milk bottles, defrosted banana puree, and more wipes, I stifled a yawn and closed my eyes for a milli-moment. My left eye twitched, begging me for more time in the deep, dark cavern of slumber. *Maybe tonight will be the night.*

An hour later, we were packed up into the car and finally on our way. Why on earth it takes so long to get ready when we are only going fifteen minutes down the road! When we pull into the underground carpark, I plead silently for a spot in the limited number of weatherproof parks (it was pouring rain) and was delighted to see a car with its reverse lights on. Yes! Someone was looking out for me today. It made dragging the pram, nappy bag and kids out of the car so much easier. I could almost smell the aroma of coffee drifting down from upstairs.

We arrived at the gate to the squeals and screaming of other families just like us. Babies crawled after their siblings. Toddlers spilled their mini-milkshakes and babycinos. Kids fought over the one superman outfit. Prams were rocked by mothers looking as tired and drained as me.

I gladly paid the fee, and we pushed through the gate to the only type of freedom I would experience that day. To the naked eye of a childless bystander, this place looked like a variation of hell on earth, but for those of us in the thick of this early parenting phase, environments like this can save our sanity. I waved to Penny, the beautiful young musician who came here once or twice a week to entertain the children. She would soon have children of her own. She revealed to me in the years to come that she used to see me coming into *Green Bean* and hoped she would be as together and calm as me when she became a mother. Ha-ha! If only I had known this was the vibe I was giving out, as it felt quite the opposite!

My coffee arrived hot. Delivered to my sticky table, I closed my eyes and breathed in the moment of pause. My baby had just crapped her nappy and my toddler was about to come hurtling down the steep, steel slippery slide, so my minutes were numbered and I would have to grapple with the change room. But somehow, amidst the chaos, everything seemed a little more manageable.

I slurped away, grateful for the break from the home front, and with a sense of comfort that others just like me were doing precisely the same thing.

In writing this book, I wanted to openly recognise the relentlessness of this phase of motherhood. For me, this was my toughest and most 'spaceless' stage of all. I want to reassure mothers currently in this stage that, although making time for yourself may seem an impossible undertaking, little cheats and shortcuts can free you from the barracks –even when you have the kids in tow. These generally involve access to an area where your toddler is safe to run around, filled with lots of toys and age-appropriate equipment and without you having to constantly chase after them.

Preferably with a gate and a lock.

PAUSE PROMPT

FIND YOUR VERSION OF 'GREEN BEAN' AND DON'T BE AFRAID TO GRAVITATE TOWARDS IT ON DESPERATE DAYS.

The combination of toddler and newborn is a bloody challenge. Running after one, breastfeeding the other. Hoping the toddler doesn't wake up the baby, or the baby doesn't wake up the toddler. Constantly wiping their bums and lugging around a filthy nappy bag slung over a second-hand pram covered in spew and shit. Trying to adjust to a new routine that is never going to grow roots and hold in any one place. The days are long, and the nights are longer.

Permission Note

I am not superhuman. I openly admit that
I need saving every now and then.

✦

Chapter 15

Sanctity In Solitude

"Doing nothing often leads to the
very best of something."

Winnie the Pooh

One Saturday, I felt inspired by an interview I read with author and mother Tara Moss[9] about how she discovered joy and fulfilment in her two vintage caravans. She described them as her happy place, her special small spaces in which to escape. She admitted vintage caravans are not for everyone, however her overall message was for women to stop trying to 'have it all' and instead 'have *your* all'. I loved this little analogy, and I popped it into my hand-woven basket of sentiment nestled against the notion of 'surrendering to motherhood'.

Just let it all go and see what pops to the surface. I could do that. Couldn't I?

Letting my guard down, I granted myself permission to slow down enough to reflect on my situation in life, not only as a new mother but also as a unique human identity. How I used to love my own company, even more than the company of my closest friends and family members. Sure, I was a chatterbox who liked to bubble around socialising, but the magic of alone time was a sacred vantage where I could restore my energy and lean into my true essence. I lamented the lack of space in my current lifestyle to claim even a few minutes of this valuable pastime and decided that now was the time to reclaim old habits.

I took the first opening I could find. It was a Saturday morning in September and, after ensuring that Glen could look after the girls for a couple of hours, I jumped onto the opportunity before I could talk myself out of it. I was going out.

Somewhere.

Anywhere.

Alone.

The spring day was bright and sunny. I ditched my phone, pulled a backpack of books and journals across my shoulders and decided to take a nice leisurely stroll over to the local botanical gardens. The walk took roughly fifteen minutes, and each step felt like a new beginning. Taking in the fresh air like it was my first breath, I felt a sense of unfathomable freedom. It had been years since I had taken the liberty of a simple walk on my own, without a pram out front or toddler tantrum along the way. How simple and yet how magical. On arrival at the garden gates, I deliberately avoided the busy area near the kids' playground and duck pond. Instead, I diverted myself to a quiet and deserted pathway that led to an opening with two large gum trees and a low wooden bench.

Feeling like a character from my favourite childhood book series 'The Magic Faraway Tree' by Enid Blyton, I propped myself onto the bench and lay on my back. I allowed myself the time to slowly breathe in the delightful scent of eucalyptus whilst softly closing my eyes. A peaceful wave of relaxation and release broke gently over me and cleared my mind of rushing thoughts and anxious checklists. After a while, I lifted myself up and grabbed my journal and pen, scribbling passionately about how I was feeling and how nurtured my spirit felt immersed in nature.

In this moment on the bench, I am Tehla and Tehla alone, entitled to soak up the solitude and serenity and just be. I am making it my mandate to savour every last moment like my life depends on it.

I continued to breathe in the energy of the great big gums as I felt myself physically shifting on the inside. It was like I was realigning with an old part of myself that had been temporarily lost and forgotten. It was like a reunion with a long-lost friend.

After about an hour and a half, I walked back home with a renewed sense of optimism and energy and the inner comfort that my children and husband would benefit immensely from this as well. I felt grounded, connected and even joyous. My mouth formed a wide-brimmed smile as I realised how simple my solo rendezvous had been, and yet how uplifting and stimulating.

I returned to the family fray with surprising optimism about making dinner. Who would have thought?

For some mothers, it might be a walk in the gardens or on

the beach, for others a quiet coffee and magazine to themselves, a yoga session or a bushwalk. Maybe a swim in the ocean or a book on a bench.

According to psychotherapist and mental strength author Amy Morin[10], there are volumes of studies touting the benefits of solitude. She outlines five 'science-backed' reasons that stem from evidence-based research into the field. These include increases in empathy, productivity, creativity, mental strength and capacity for planning your life. She reminds us that solitary skills take practice, but over time we can feel more comfortable simply being by ourselves. Our compassion towards others can also grow when we set time aside for solitude. As little as ten minutes each day is all that is required.

The concept of *A Mother's Space* includes any activity where you can stretch your limbs, restore your centre and pursue a pastime that lights up your spirit and soul in solitude. To just be, without expectation or judgement. Author Nikki Gemmell[11] describes these opportunities as her 'little moments' when she can take back control of her life.

"… and suddenly when children arrived, I lost control of so many aspects of my life that writing—those little moments when I'd dash upstairs and sit in front of a laptop—was the only time when I felt in control. It was my little pocket of selfishness, in a way. I felt lit, it was a real balm when I was sitting there at my computer, and that gave me strength to get through all the exhaustion and nipples hurting because of the breastfeeding …"

As mothers, we can quickly become short-circuited to the practice of 'doing nothing'. We simply forget how to 'do' what we learned as kids when we watched television for hours on end, sat on our beds daydreaming, relinquished our duties or chatted in a park with our friends as the sun set before us. Where have those times gone?

> Do we need to hone the muscle of 'doing nothing' again to get back into practice?

How can the other members of our household (like our partner) support us along this journey? How can our own children buy into the ideology that 'mummy-time' is sacred and essential, and absolutely vital to the smooth running of our family home? Every member of our tribe needs to be crystal clear about the importance and benefits of our spiritual space. Without it, it's like surviving a swim against a rising river of rapids full of crocodiles. Possible, but not probable.

PAUSE PROMPT
THREE TIPS FOR EMBRACING SOLITUDE
AND THE ART OF 'DOING NOTHING'

Sitting in your own company alone can be confronting, but also liberating. Embrace your own version of 'solo magic' and build your awareness of the positive impact it can have on your patience levels, vitality and self-confidence.

Tip One:
Know you are worthy and deserving of this time.
I often feel we resist our alone time as mothers because we do not feel worthy or deserving of this time to ourselves. This can be attributed to guilt, lack of time, or that our needs are not high enough up the chain in our family hierarchy. Whatever the reason is for you, it is time for you to weed your garden of insecurity and plant in your seeds of self-worth. Close your eyes and visualise these tiny seeds in the palm of your hand.

Know that these seeds require such a deep sense of love and nurturing that only *you* can provide for them. Tend to them with care. Imagine you are planting them into the rich soil of mother earth and water them each day with a tenderness you would give to your own children and family members. Sometimes all we need to do is shift the lens of care from others to ourselves and suddenly realise that our own self-worth and desires have not disappeared. They just need our loving attention to come back into the forefront of our life.

Tip Two:

Enlist family buy in and support for your solitude.

Doing nothing truly is a team effort! Once you have overcome your own doubts around self-worth, including the realisation that your 'solo magic' is right there waiting for you, it is so important that the rest of your family (or at the very least your partner) is fully on board with this and they are supportive and encouraging of your personal needs for space. I am not going to lie to you. This can be a very challenging step, but often it is our own insecurities around self-worthiness that hinder this process (which is why *Tip One* is at the top of this list!).

It took around three or four years for me to truly feel supported and unhindered in my own processes of claiming space to myself and overcoming my guilt for doing so. But once my husband was on board, he also helped me educate our girls about the importance of 'mummy's space'. Slowly but surely, every member of our family now understands to respect my space when I take myself for a walk, or run myself a bath with the door locked, or retreat to my special room in the house for some down time.

Know that this is not always a linear process. It is circular and can feel like you are making progress one step forwards for every two steps backwards. One of the kids might get sick, or your husband might suddenly need to work, or there might be a fire in the kitchen (okay, I'm embellishing now, but you get my point!).

Like life, finding space as a mother is not perfect. A 'perfect storm' perhaps, but otherwise the very opposite of perfect and ordered!

Tip Three:

Be prepared to spontaneously surrender into 'solo magic' at any time!

Disclaimer: Opportunities to immerse yourself in solitude are not delivered on a silver platter! Had I realised this early on in motherhood, I would have saved myself a lot of heartache and pain. In the early days of parenting, it is unlikely your partner will use extrasensory perception (ESP) or telepathy to understand it is time for you to take a break. Your baby sure won't tell you either. If we return to *Tip One: Know you are worthy and deserving of this time*, a big part of creating space for solitude in your life is about taking ownership of your own inner wellbeing and alerting those closest to you that you need and deserve some time out. When an opportunity for sacred space in solitude offers itself up, take it by the horns and don't let go!

No regrets allowed.

Permission Note

I seek space in solitude to return to my innermost thoughts and self.

Chapter 16

My Journal, My Friend

*"Journalling is
like whispering
to one's self
and listening
at the same time."*

Mina Murray

I often daydream about my old bedroom as a teenager. It was my private space of retreat and rest with everything just the way I liked it. Study desk against the window. Single bed in the corner with my favourite white lace doona cover gifted by my Great Aunt. Super-comfy pillow. Ceiling-high built-in wardrobes with secret areas hidden within. Fairy table. Yes, you heard right. A table dedicated to my *fairy collection*. What hasn't changed since my teenage years is that I always had a diary, either dream or personal, next to my bed or close by. Writing and journalling have been important parts of my life since I was about twelve years old and that continues now, thirty years later. The seeds for this book started as pages and pages of scribble in my journals and notebooks before the words took on any shape suitable for a published book!

Years ago, I upgraded to a queen bed with the onset of marriage and kids. But selfishly I sometimes yearn for that little single bed with all its simplicity and solitude, where I would read until all hours of the night, then spread out and sleep until I woke by natural forces.

The practice of journalling and keeping a diary has been one of the main constants in my life. The more regularly I journal, the easier I find it to move through life and make sense of my place in it. In contrast, when I don't proactively dedicate space to journalling, I feel restless, dubious and laden with self-doubt. One priority of my daily ritual is to keep my journal tucked safely into my handbag so I can whip it out whenever the call to write comes on. I can also consult it for comfort and reassurance if times get tough or if I happen to have a day of doubt. My relationship with my journals and words has been a powerful and strong force for courage and self-belief, especially on the days I felt like giving up. A page of my journal from early 2015 went something like this:

I love looking back over my entries—on the hard days it provides confidence in myself that I can do this, whatever 'this' is, and on the good days it helps reinforce the excitement and the sheer exhilaration of having my own words as a loyal and trusted friend, a companion of sorts.

Overall, it helps me to believe in myself.

One of my favourite things to journal is letters to my girls. It is so interesting to observe the types of messages I have written to them, and that by addressing them in a letter format somehow increases the impact of my words. I have hundreds of them since they were born and plan to collate them all one day and give them each their 'book of letters', perhaps on a milestone birthday. An excerpt from a letter to my eldest daughter when she was two years old reveals how excited and proud I am of the little person she is becoming.

You are now 2 years and 4 months and not a little baby anymore. A 'big girl' as you put it! You have certainly embraced the 'terrible twos' and tantrums, but overall your Daddy and I are just loving watching you grow more and more each day. You have a good understanding that Mummy has a baby in her tummy and you pat my belly often and talk about the baby to others. At day-care, the girls have told me that you are very good with the babies in the room and have become quite gentle and 'motherly' towards them. You still get protective of Mummy when I'm holding another baby, but hopefully that will change once we have a baby in the house permanently!

If you feel resistant or put off by the practice of 'journalling' or 'diary-keeping', I invite you to consider a practice such as daily gratitude, which is more list and prompt-based as opposed to free writing of feelings. The simple act of allowing yourself a moment of discerning reflection at the start, middle or end of your day can be so rewarding and self-affirming. I encourage you to give it a go! Some benefits of journalling and 'jotting' include:

- It is yours and yours alone, like a private conversation with an old friend
- It becomes a record, a moment in time and a confidante
- Reading back over and reflecting on your own words in the years after you write them can deliver powerful messages for your present life
- Learning from your past self
- Identifying patterns and affirming what is working or not working in your life
- Letting out your fears and worries without judgement
- Recording the precious moments that we often forget as mothers (because we are too busy mothering!)
- Your journal or notebook becomes your source of inner power, strength and validation of your life's path

The relationship you develop with your notebook, journal or gratitude diary can reveal thoughts, ideas and feelings you didn't even know existed. If used regularly, it can help fuse together these ideas and feelings and identify meaningful patterns in your life's journey. One of the most powerful journals I kept was in the year 2015. It was a hardback diary designed by Toni Carmine Salerno titled *Inspiration Journal:*

My Thoughts, Inspirations and Reflections'. I still have it and refer back to it often. Every page offered a beautiful but subtle quote or message at the bottom, inspiring me to write something even on the days I felt powerless to do so. My entry on the final page of this journal summarises the connectedness I felt to it.

> *We have now entered 2015, a new year of opportunity, of faith in life, of kids and fun and hopefully a lot better health for our whole family. And this, sadly, is the final page of this journal. I feel quite anxious about not being able to write in it. It has helped heal me so much over these months. In a way, it represents to me who I really am, and reassures me of the goodness I hold and will hope to continue to hold in the coming year. THANK YOU.*

I felt an extremely powerful and strong bond with the pages of this particular notebook. On reflection, it was *the* journal that truly stripped back all the layers of me and my ego and revealed to me just who I was and who I was becoming. This journal, in essence, captured what was to become my very real transformation in 2016, the year I finally built up the courage to shake up my career and follow my path of teaching yoga and writing.

PAUSE PROMPT
AN (OPTIONAL) ASSIGNMENT

Take yourself to the closest newsagent, bookshop or gift shop. Open your mind as you walk in and pick out the first journal or notepad that your eyes alight upon. Buy it. Take it back to your car. Write your name and date on the inside cover.

Now, you are ready. You have a journal, and you have made a start. What you do with it next is up to you. Treat it like an old friend, and it will never let you down.

Permission Note

There is nothing in my day that I can't
journal my way out of.

Chapter 17

Space For Grief - Part 1

"Those we love don't go away. They walk beside us
every day. Unseen, unheard, but always near. Still
loved, still missed, and very dear."

Alex MacLean

'There's not a lot more we can do,' said the veterinarian. 'We
might have to call it a day.'

Pressing the phone closer to my ear where I stood
outside the city library, I frowned, assuming I must have
misheard him.

'I thought you said he had just eaten too much, and that
he would be coming home today?'

'Yes, that's what we thought initially, when you brought
him in two weeks ago. But after further tests, ultrasounds and
examinations, we have discovered Dexter's heart is drowning
in blood. We suspect he has terminal cancer. The pressure
around his heart is just too much to operate on, and even then,
there is not a lot of hope for recovery. You will need to come in
so you can say goodbye.'

Choking back tears, I reflected on the night before. How

he lost control of his little bony legs, and how we had to hold him up on the lawn outside so he could manage to do his business. How I carefully moved him with his doggy bed into our bedroom, right next to me so I could reach out and stroke or pat him reassuringly, and so we could monitor him closely. And how, as soon as morning arrived, and the vet opened up for the day, I rushed him over to see what was wrong.

Deep down, I think I knew something more sinister was at play, as I didn't even brush my teeth or hair on the way out of the house. We had been at the vet's two weeks earlier, and the prognosis was that he had overeaten, putting a strain on his stomach. We were sent home with medication to help his digestion and didn't think much more of it. Dexter then came with us to my father-in-law's seventieth birthday celebrations, a three-hour drive away. He spent the weekend exhibiting all the classic signs of his typical, energetic, jumping Jack Russell self.

This time, two weeks later, they took a look at him and said they weren't sure what was going on. I needed to leave him with them while they ran some additional tests. Obviously, he was in a lot more pain and discomfort than we originally thought.

I visualised his cute little face in my mind, his long eyelashes and loyal eyes. Those eyes had followed me protectively for eleven years now, through each of my pregnancies and the arrival in the house of our baby girls in 2011 and 2014 respectively. He was my first 'baby' and earned the title of 'shadow' because he walked behind me wherever I went. From the moment we brought him home as an eight-week-old pup, he always sought my attention or approval, and vibed off my energy.

He was more than a dog. He was my loyal friend, my companion, and in my times of struggle, the only other living thing in this world who truly knew me. We had a special bond. In many ways, Dex witnessed my highest highs and my lowest lows. I had a Jack Russell terrier called 'Tex' growing up, and he lived to be over twenty years old, so I thought we still had over a decade of Dexter left.

I was wrong.

After hanging up the phone from the vet, I frantically scrolled my recent phone numbers until I landed on Glen's number, fingers shaking, hoping he would see it in the cinema session he had taken the girls to. Thankfully, he picked up first go.

'I've heard back from the vet's, mate,' I whispered. 'We need to meet there now so we can say goodbye to Dexie.'

Silence on the other end. Like myself, Glen could not believe this was happening. Our boy, our Dexie boy, was dying, and we both struggled to comprehend the sudden nature of his departure from our world.

'Okay, mate,' he finally replied. 'We'll be there in twenty minutes.'

I arrived at the vet's first and rushed in to see him. A surge of urgency swept through me. I *had* to hold him. *Now.* Luckily, the vet was at the reception desk waiting for us and took me right in. Seeing me, Dexter's eyes lit up and his tail wagged ever so gently. *I'm sorry*, his eyes said. I wanted to tell you. *I'm sorry to be causing such stress.*

I heard Glen and the girls arrive and went out to get them. The collective emotion was overwhelming. We kept saying how we couldn't believe this was happening. We each had a turn cuddling him and holding him, and Glen and I agreed I would stay with him while he was put to sleep.

I cradled him in my arms as he took his final breath, saying over and over to him two words that just kept releasing from my mouth, '*thank you, thank you, thank you*'.

The energy left his body, and he went limp.

I have since learned from listening to an interview with acclaimed animal naturopath Ruth Hatten that our pets often take on and absorb our energies, particularly those affecting us negatively, and that this can manifest as disease in their own bodies. They willingly make this sacrifice, for us, their beloved owners. Hearing this made me feel so guilty. It was a logical explanation as to why Dexter may have left his body earlier than his predisposed genetic makeup.

We trudged back to the car without Dexter. It was so hard to believe he wasn't just staying over at the vets, that he was never coming home. Life suddenly felt so empty. It was like our family unit had lost a limb and we had become lopsided.

'I can't go home yet,' I said to Glen. 'The house will be so empty and quiet without him.'

We headed to the beach and Glen and I sat solemnly while we watched the girls run down to the water. At ages seven and five, they understood what had happened but didn't quite realise the finality of it all, that the family dog they had known their whole lives would not be coming home.

In the days and weeks after Dexter passed, I saw him everywhere and yet nowhere. I waited for his barking to wake us up in the morning, only to realise it wouldn't be starting off our day. People knocked on our door without us knowing as 'doorbell Dexie' no longer alerted us of a visitor or stranger on our doorstop. I pulled up in the garage and waited to see his four little paws pacing anxiously from under the door to the backyard. He always welcomed us with raucous barking, jumping up with excitement every time we arrived home, even if we only popped down the street for five minutes to grab milk.

I could only pause slightly to process the loss I felt before one of the kids started yelling or crying or arguing with the other. The demands of family life pressed on, the running from school to after-school activities, to preschool and day-care, to parties, to work, to the grocery store, to medical appointments, to family commitments.

The deeper grieving for Dexter came in the months after, coinciding with a three-month road trip. The months where we clocked up over 12,000 km travelling around at random, in the outback of our beautiful country and right up to the top of Queensland. Those long days in the van caught me off guard, as I looked out the window at the red dirt and dust, and the striking bottle green of the trees against the earth.

In those moments, he came to me like a vision in my mind's eye. I saw his face and felt his presence and his love for us all, and I allowed the tears to not only well up, but to pour forth, in joy of the memories and in sorrow for the totality of the loss. Sometimes it was a long landscape, other times a song or photo memory on my phone.

I found space for it. I made space for it. I *prioritised* space for the grieving to come. And then I *allowed* it to flow.

PAUSE PROMPT
PETS AT PEACE POEM

"If it should be, that I grow frail and weak,
And pain should keep me from my sleep,
Then, you must do what must be done
For this, the last battle can't be won.

You will be sad, I understand,
Don't let your grief then stay your hand,
For this day, more than the rest,
Your love and friendship stand the test.

We've had so many happy years,
What is to come can hold no fears,
You'd not want me to suffer, so,
When the time comes, please let me go.
Smile, for we walked together, for a little while."

Tracy M. Johnson

Chapter 18

Space For Grief - Part 2

"You were more than our Pop
You were our guide and our rock
Dearly beloved
And never ever forgotten."

Tehla Jane Bower, Ode to Pop (1927 – 2019)

We arrived home from our 12,000 km trip, finally coming to grips with Dexter's departure. A few weeks later, my beloved Pop died. We had been warned his leukemia had worsened and that he was back in hospital after yet another fall. Pop hated hospitals and being sick. He was a tough old patient, but he wouldn't have had it any other way!

The week before he died, the local newspaper in Wollongong ran a front-page story about his Army service in Japan as a nineteen-year-old. It was touching for him and Nan, but also bittersweet as he had been seeking this recognition for over seventy years.

Losing Pop hit me like a seismic wave. I missed his voice, his stories and his chocolate addiction. It was horrible to think this, but I was so grateful he waited for us to get home from our trip before leaving his body. To have the privilege of saying goodbye, not once but multiple times over. To watch his eyes light up as we shared the stories of our travels. No matter how remote and tiny the outback town, he had his own version of a story about it, as he and Nan had travelled the country many times over.

He knew every pub, every landscape, every waterway and every highway. Years before our girls were born, he begged Glen and I to travel outback with him and Nan so he could show us the sights and 'shoot some rabbits'. I wasn't so keen on the shooting, but my heart sighed with regret that we were too busy with our work and careers to commit to having a few weeks away from the office. If only I could go back in time, I would take that trip with him any day of the week!

As I watched him deteriorate, I longed for the little things we used to share. A beer at the Friday night raffles, a prized tomato or lettuce from his famous veggie patch, a roast dinner prepared only the way Nan made it, followed by her sticky date pudding drenched in sauce, cream and ice cream. I craved one of his long-winded embellished stories about crocodiles or hunting or camping using only an old tarp flung over two trees on a creek bed. Nan correcting the details.

After the funeral, I heard Pop's voice everywhere. I wanted to bottle it up, so I didn't forget the intonations and distinctive Aussie twang. I visited Nan and the house felt so empty, so quiet, and I realised how his energy and presence filled up every room. He owned his personal space with conviction and surety, and all his strong opinions about life reverberated through our family lineage for better or for worse. It was like a huge vacuum had sucked up all his 'Pop-ness' and I couldn't find it anymore.

Now that I was back in the daily grind of school and work routines, I seemed to forget all the lessons I learnt on the road about allowing the grief to come when it needed to come. I let fear get in the way again.

How was I supposed to openly allow my feelings and emotions to come on cue when I had the daily responsibilities of being a mother? My children were reliant on me. I couldn't let them down. I couldn't forget to feed them, take them to school or be actively present with them, as I liked to pride myself on. I was the wisdom holder of the family's daily calendar. One slip up or missed appointment, excursion item or library bag could create a domino effect and order would become chaos. I couldn't allow myself to be seen by them as unreliable, or weak or excessively emotional. *Could I?*

But then, perhaps that was supposed to happen? By making way for grieving the loss of a pet or family member, aren't we encouraged to embrace the messiness of life in all its cycles and imperfections? Revealing to our children that mummy doesn't have her shit together all the time is perfectly okay. It is okay to break down and weep out loud for the loss and grief we are experiencing. It is okay to do it in real time, without bottling it up until we explode with unreleased emotion.

Visiting his grave one afternoon, I told Pop all about our girls and how they were growing up. I told him how much I wished he could see them just one more time, and how great his garden was doing with Nan tending to it. I struggled to keep the tears back even though I had the girls with me. They weren't being too patient. I guess I can't blame them—not a lot for kids to do at a cemetery. Behind us, about a hundred galahs took flight, making so much racket and circling over us. I received an instant knowing that this was a sign from Pop, responding to my stories and updates in his usual fashion— loudly and with plenty of cheer! I felt immediate comfort. After this encounter, whenever I see a galah, I know Pop is close by.

PAUSE PROMPT
EMBRACE IT ALL

Of all the years since having children, 2019 was the one that resulted in the biggest triumphs, loss and growth as a family. We lost our dear dog Dexter. We ventured spontaneously out into some of the remotest parts of our country, and I lost the closest paternal influence in my life next to my own father, my beloved Pop. There was sorrow, joy, excitement, pride, and a special seed planted for a new beginning to come in 2022. Learning to embrace it all and knowing these events were teaching and guiding me along the pathway of my life gave me great comfort amidst the discomfort. Writing about it helped the healing, too.

Have you found yourself struggling to grieve openly for a lost loved one due to the daily demands of motherhood? Do not be afraid to let your feelings flow forth, no matter if the kids are around or not. This is an important part of our experience in life, not just as mothers but as human beings. By unashamedly opening your own emotional vault you send the message to your children (and yourself) that feelings such as sadness and sorrow are a normal response to loss. If the dinner doesn't get made or the dishes don't get done, or you have to take a day off work – give yourself permission to do whatever is needed at this time and truly feel in to your human experience.

Permission Note

I prioritise space to grieve for
my loss. This is an important
part of my healing.

Part 3
DEEPER DISCOVERING

Chapter 19

The Mum Cave
— Creating Space At Home

"Creating a sacred space is a simple yet powerful act. It is a place devoted to the part of you that whispers, calls and yearns."

Rebecca Campbell

Do you have a hiding space at home where you know you won't be interrupted, even if only for a few minutes?

For me, it is the back office or the trampoline. I once had a nice lengthy phone conversation with my best friend Danielle from the trampoline in our front yard. Just me, lying on my back on the trampoline, looking up at the clouds without my kids.

'What are you doing?' she asked.

'Hiding from the kids,' I replied honestly. 'I just need a moment, otherwise I'm going to lose my shit at them, and it's not even their fault.'

Some mothers lock themselves in the bathroom. Others hide under the office desk or behind the curtains in the bedroom. I can find myself anywhere from the trampoline to the bedroom cupboard, my car in the garage, the back room or locked in the bathroom. Essentially, anywhere that my children are not.

Mummy's retreat room, 'she shed', 'ladies lair', 'mum cave', the secret area under the stairs. Whatever we name it, I believe that creating a sacred space for yourself within your home is an important piece of the puzzle to claiming some regular time out as a mother. Erika Kotite, author of *'She Sheds'*, describes it beautifully as 'your own little piece of heaven'.

> *"As women, we handle a heavy load of responsibility: jobs, marriage, children, ageing parents, household chores, and social obligations. Days will go by after which we ask ourselves, 'Have I had one minute alone, in the quiet, to myself?' She sheds are a refuge of comfort, there for however you want to use them. A she shed is for you and you alone."*

I love this so much and have a dream of one day creating my own unique restoration in the back yard. The guys have their man sheds and private garages to hide in, so what's stopping us from creating our own version?

Baby steps first. For now, I have experimented with finding space inside my home. The first retreat room I created for myself came about in late 2018, and I need to be perfectly honest about this, during a time where my marriage was a little shaky. If there was any benefit to this period, it forced me to prioritise finding space in the home where I could be alone. I took a good look at the only spare room in the house (it was a guestroom, office, storage room and library all in one) and suddenly saw potential. Separated from the other bedrooms in the house, it felt more private. It featured a foldout bed that backed up as a groovy makeshift couch, an office desk and a dusty bookshelf. I added my personal touches to it. Yoga mat in the corner, fresh books and inspiring materials for the bookcase against the far wall, work desk positioned against the window to take advantage of the garden view and ocean in the distance. Day by day, week by week, the room took on a character and personality of its own, uplifting me with a little moment of magic each time I stepped in and closed the door behind me.

> My retreat room became an instant source of sanctitude and relaxation. I would enter with a grateful sigh and breathe in the peace and quiet, taking a good moment or two to appreciate each cycle of breath.

It was more than a physical room of the house. It was *sacred*. International spiritual teacher and mystic Rebecca Campbell describes the creation of these types of sacred places as *'simple yet powerful'*, devoted to the parts of us that whisper, yearn and call out to our inner selves. She believes the more attention and care we place on our special little spaces, the more fuelled with sacred energy they become. By tending to it regularly, you can develop a deeper connection with the parts of you that are inviting you back into yourself.

Continue to water these parts and feel your inner light begin to shine through once more.

As the months went on, I was called to my mum space more and more. Retreating here, closing the door, rolling out my yoga mat, I listened to music I hadn't heard in forever. By early 2019, everyone in the household knew this room as 'mummy's retreat room', and most of the time, respected my privacy when the door was closed. *Note that this is a lot easier the older the children are. When they are toddlers or pre-schoolers, there's not much keeping them away, least of all a closed door (which can oftentimes lead to the opposite effect)!*

It's all about finding what works for you based on your unique family composition and the layout of your home. Forever changing and shifting, what works now may not work in a few months' or years' time. Try not to get over-attached. Simply appreciate what you are creating. See how it serves you, the more love, care and respect you give to it.

Treat it as a sacred thread that is connected to you always, but continually evolving with you. Maybe it is a quiet corner in your bedroom, or a windowsill drenched in sunlight out of the reach of little arms and fingers. Find it, claim it and baptise it with your own signature pieces and vibes.

If nothing else, can you allocate three minutes and thirty seconds to listen to your favourite song, or a song that was a favourite for you growing up? Try to listen differently, not as a background noise, but to every word and intonation of the song, feel into the meaning and connect with the voice of the singer. I did this recently with Sara Bareilles' song 'Brave'. I heard a fragment of the lyrics float out of a café radio and reserved time when I was alone later on to tune in to the words and melodies. The song took on fresh meaning for me. I connected to it as a writer, being encouraged to pour words onto a page.

'Say what you wanna say
And let the words fall out
Honestly, I wanna see you be brave'

When we moved houses in early 2022, we gained so much in a beautiful new home in an equally beautiful coastal community. But something was missing for me. After weeks and months of feeling lost and at times irritated in the new home, I realised I had yet to take up my own advice and claim a little area of the house to myself!

Despite being more spacious, it was difficult to pinpoint a spot that offered privacy and pleasing aesthetics. Our new abode offered high ceilings and open plan living, but that made it a challenge to reserve a room or corner without being out in the open myself. I was working from the kitchen bench, and we had no spare bedrooms at the house. The only areas seemed to be the downstairs room, which my husband was using for his office, or the old aviary in the backyard occupied by two cute, but also filthy, bunny rabbits!

Alone in the house one day, I took a visual audit of my options. The downstairs room was crying out to me, begging me to save it from the piles of paperwork and cobwebbed corners. Guilt pervaded me, and I told myself that I couldn't do it. Glen would have nowhere to work from. A deep-down part of me, lurking around in my gullet, reminded me how much more important his work was compared to mine. More guilt. Shame. Unworthiness.

This cycle of toying around and reimagining parts of the house continued for weeks. I felt so lost and *temporary* I guess would be the best word to describe it. Eventually, my husband did his own audit of the spaces in the house and announced he was moving his office to the garage.

'I can work from anywhere, Teals.'

Seeing his old office empty, I finally gave myself permission to imagine what this room could look like. My energy shifted. I felt hopeful and excited about this little room, and the universe really started to guide me along the way. The yellow-tailed black cockatoos circled the house, landing in the trees out the front, encouraging me with their ethereal cries. The kookaburras came and perched on the fence line, their gaze directed to the inside of the room, staring at me, willing me to imagine more deeply.

I got to work, I listened in, and I dismissed the guilty, shameful, unworthy parts of me until they were but a mere whisper from a faraway place.

I purchased a little white table, matching drawers and a white chair. Don't ask me why everything had to be white! I brought all my crystals and yoga supplies down into the room and lined the box-shaped shelves with spiritual books. I hung up a lace curtain to soften the heavy, grey fabric and tones of the existing drapes. And then I did something I was not anticipating. I ordered a treatment bed (also white!).

This room not only started taking shape with inspirational pieces and sacred items for my own healing and it also became a sacred place for others seeking crystal healings, meditations, and spiritual guidance. *The Crystal Healing Room* was born! It was, and still is at the time of writing, my personal hide-out on the home front. On entering, I instantly feel at ease. The energy is loving and pure, and Glen and the girls know that when the door is shut, I need my space.

An essential element to creating your haven space within the home is the support of your partner. They help you educate the other members of your home that this area is sacred and when mummy is in there, it's her special time. Hang up a sign or put a lock on the door. Whatever helps you get that moment to yourself matters!

PAUSE PROMPT
INSPIRATION FROM THE EXPERTS

Feeling lost about where to start? A beautifully crafted hardcover book by Erika Kotite called 'She-Sheds: A DIY Guide for Huts, Hideaways, and Garden Escapes Created by Women for Women' offers so many ideas and inspiration for creating your own space at home. Unashamedly. With passion, purpose and ground rules around entering and respecting the sacred and carefully crafted space of yours. She even has a website and social media sites to match.

Check out www.sheshedliving.com for more inspiration on creating your very own private hideaway in the comfort of your home.

Permission Note

I look for opportunities in and around my home

to create a corner

or a room

into a private oasis of inspiration and joy.

Chapter 20

Sleeping Space

"Without enough sleep,
we all become tall two-year-olds."

JoJo Jensen

Lying on my back on the couch, my big belly protruding in line with my nose, I allowed my eyes to finally fall to a close. My memory of a solid sleep was beyond the recall capabilities of my foggy brain. *'I really need this today,'* I said to myself. *'Even if I just get ten minutes here in peace, it will be enough to get me through ...'*

Jinx!

Just as the corners of my mouth started to curl upwards into a lazy, sleepy smile, half a litre of water landed smack in the centre of my face, jolting me upright as I screamed out in shock. Standing in front of me with a cheeky grin and a cackling laugh to match was my two-year-old daughter. Holding her empty drink bottle up like a prize medallion, I think she was expecting praise for her calculating attempt to 'stop mummy from sleeping'. At thirty-five weeks pregnant, with a toddler who refused to sleep in the day—actually, make that day *or* night—I was bloody exhausted, with hormones raging. So, wiping the water off my face as I tried to pat my hair dry with my grubby maternity skirt, I responded by doing what any other mother in the same position might do.

I burst into tears.

I was tired and desperate.

I needed a moment to myself more than I had ever needed one. I was so anxious about the impending weeks where I would be responsible for not one, but two, human beings. And I felt utterly defeated by the tiny little blue-eyed energiser bunny in front of me, hopping up and down with glee.

How the absolute fuck am I going to pull this off if I can't get a wink of sleep? I am flailing already at this motherhood gig, and I've only got one child to deal with! What am I going to do with two of them?

I cast my mind back briefly to before I had children. For the first thirty years of my life, I opposed waking any time before 6.30 am. It just didn't feel right to my system. To rise when the stars had only just flickered their final twinkles in the night sky was like a direct message from the universe to *stay in bed, Tehla!* More often than not, it was because I hadn't gone to sleep until after midnight, reading 'just one more chapter' of a good book, staying in the bath for hours, studying or cramming for exams and scrambling to meet work or assignment deadlines. All my creative inclination and inspiration seemed to come into force just after the clock ticked past 11.00 pm!

Before I became a mother, I rarely questioned my sleeping patterns. If it was a workday, I simply pushed through the day on three hours' sleep and went to bed early that night, knowing I would have no distractions straight through. Wine and coffee were my best friends. I fuelled myself with either or both to keep going and meet my deadlines. Sleep was one of my lowest priorities. I regarded it as an unnecessary nuisance in my busy and important day. I didn't have time for sleep! Pfft!

Motherhood ensured my nocturnal comforts and sleep-in freedoms were sucked down the plughole with the rose-scented bathwater of my late-night soaks! Now I woke every few hours to the screaming of my baby or the painful engorgement of my leaking teats. Or I lay back languidly in the feeding chair at 4.00 am wondering what day it was, scrolling through meaningless social media feeds of mothers who looked like they were getting a lot more sleep than I was. And what is it with 4.00 am? I feel that every baby is pre-programmed to wake at this exact time—too early to start the day after a feed, but also too late to get back to sleep before the day kicks in.

Sweet, deep sleep moved swiftly and dramatically up my priority chain.

My second baby girl arrived shortly after the 'drink bottle incident on the lounge'. Here I was with a toddler who hated sleeping, a two-week-old baby with bronchiolitis and a truckload of clients needing submissions written.

My nightly sleep average dropped to a lifetime low of two hours of sleep, every night, for six months (or about 180 nights). Much of that was spent on the floor of my baby's bedroom. I lay on the carpet next to her little cot with its heavyweight books wedged under the two legs of the bedhead for efficient drainage of her nasal passage and Eustachian tubes. I anxiously watched for the rise and fall of her chest. My nervous system and adrenals were shot to smithereens. Once or twice a month during this period, we found ourselves in the emergency department at the hospital where the paediatric doctors inserted little tubes into both nostrils and manually cleared the passage so she could breathe—and ultimately sleep.

After one such hospital visit, I knew I had to take some radical action to save my sleep and sanity so I could continue to care for my children. I would lose focus when driving the car and panicked about falling asleep at the wheel. I felt on edge every evening in anticipation of another sleepless night. I wondered how all the other mothers out there managed to do it. Why did I feel so alone and lost? Or was every other mother just as tired and anxious and feeling the same?

Research by The Sleep Foundation in the United States reports that the average new mother receives approximately six hours sleep a night[12]. I don't know where they got their numbers from, but I'm calling bullshit on this. Unless I'm hanging in the wrong circles of mothers, I have never come across a mother who averaged that kind of sleep duration in their first six weeks of bringing a child into the world for the first time. I would be delighted to be proved otherwise!

Whether you have children who are newborn, toddler, teething, sick or not sick, your sleep cycles have likely changed since becoming a mother. Ultimately, the sleep patterns of your children have a direct correlation with your quality of sleep. I still catch myself sleeping with one eye open some nights in case my girls yell out. My youngest still has a tendency to wet the bed from time to time and my eldest still has a fear of the dark and of falling asleep in general.

The truth is, if we are chronically sleep deprived as mothers, we simply cannot help those who need us the most. There will be days, months, and cycles when we find it impossible to catch up on sleep. When we are in this stage, we want to knock out any mother who tells us they are getting ample sleep and feel well rested! I had many times in the early stages of motherhood where I gave up and believed there was no solution to the sleep deprivation dilemma. I read about the Dalai Lama's sleep habits for optimal health and spiritual functioning, and how he goes to bed at 8.30 pm every night and rises at 3.30 am[13]. These times were referenced in 2012 and I believe today he rises even earlier! My sleep patterns were consistent with his 'waking' hour, but the 'bedtime' hour was nowhere close!

Okay, let's face it, the sleeping patterns of the Dalai Lama should not be our benchmark as sleep-deprived mothers! Back to more realistic goals …

One random day when my youngest was about nine months old, I chose to surrender to sleep. It was no circadian rhythm cycle, and it was not endorsed by a leading Buddhist monk, but I surrendered up everything *except* sleep. I knew if I didn't, my life was going to fall apart. Around the same time, I heard of a mother from Sydney who died from exhaustion. I cried for her family but also because I saw my life reflected in hers. I then read about a study[14] by the Sleep Research Society in *Sleep* journal that validated the correlations between lack of sleep and mortality rates, and my mind was made up.

I had to start taking my own sleep seriously.

It wasn't easy, but I gave it my best shot. If Avah fell asleep in the car on our way to the shops (or anywhere), I would pull over somewhere quiet, carefully turn off the ignition, and close my eyes too. At home, if my eldest was at day-care, as soon as Avah fell asleep in the middle of the day, I fought the urge to tidy up, check social media or catch up on work emails (this took so much effort!). I curled up on the couch. Unless it was the day-care phone number calling, I ignored all phone calls too.

The late Dr Wayne W. Dyer presented a lecture in 2012 titled '*The Miracle of Being*', that I stumbled upon on a podcast one morning.

One particular topic towards the end of the recording caught my attention. It referenced the subconscious mind, which is the part of our mind apparently responsible for 96% of what we do in our day. Dyer speaks of the importance of the time of day where the subconscious mind shifts and 'launches' into the more uncontrollable unconscious mind, and the affect this has on our mental programming for the following day.

He argues that the last five minutes of our day,
before we go to bed, are the most important five
minutes of the day, and that these five minutes
influence everything you will face upon waking
the next day.

It got me thinking about my own daily mindful practices and the impact that they have on my quality of sleep and my morning mood. If I can head to bed at a reasonable hour with a cup of chamomile tea and read something uplifting for five to ten minutes, it makes the world of difference to my energy levels and motivation the next day. It is not always realistic with restless children, but five small minutes made me believe I could do it!

I am a big fan of spiritual author and motivational speaker Gabby Bernstein, and I listened to the tail end of a talk she gave about the importance of healthy sleep habits. Bernstein believes a lack of sleep can seriously block our personal power, creativity and intuition—diminishing our energy field and overall state of wellbeing.

Feeling motivated by her talk, I gave myself permission to invest in some fresh, beautiful (and slightly expensive but worth it) linen sheets. I upgraded my old pre-loved pillow from years ago to a fluffy stain-free plumper option and cleansed our bedroom with a stick of sage. I announced that all technological devices were now banned from our bedrooms, especially at bedtime. And I started having regular baths just before bed, which seemed to help calm down my system. Would the girls barge into the bathroom while I was having a bath? Of course they would! But even if I experienced ten short seconds of warmth and peace *before* this happened, it was worth it. Did my new bedtime ritual stop my girls from waking up or yelling out during the night? No way! But I felt better equipped to deal with any midnight distractions that might occur.

We cannot control teething, bedwetting, nightmares, temperatures, ear infections or spew bugs. But starting the night off well-intentioned and placing *value* on *my* sleep patterns shifted my perspective and gave me the support I needed for a more quality, purposeful type of sleep.

PAUSE PROMPT
SLEEP HABIT HACK

Allow yourself to think differently about your daily sleep regime and invite new perspectives in. What could you do to improve or increase the quality of sleep you get, even if this only happens once a week? Aim for tiny steps in your sleep progress. If one night out of fourteen is better than the rest, focus in on that one. Above all, be kind to yourself! The nights where you are up and down like a yo-yo tending to teething toddlers, crying babies or bed-wetting children need to be written off. A small tweak in your sleep routine can be transformative. Sitting with a hot cup of herbal tea and no smartphone in reach for just ten minutes in your bedroom before bed can slow your racing mind and help your body prepare for a promising slumber.

Permission Note

My bedroom is my haven for rest. I intentionally shower it with love, fresh air, fresh sheets and fluffy slippers.

Chapter 21

A Night Away, For One

"Sometimes you just need a break.
In a beautiful place. Alone.
To figure everything out."

Anonymous

Do you love your own company? I do! I love spending time with myself. I'm often known as a bubbly, chatty kind of person, but deep down I'm quite a private person. I relish in the stillness and silence that being in my own company offers.

In my years adapting to motherhood, I've found myself escaping for a night away occasionally to catch up on sleep or just remind myself of who I am. Like anything, the first time I did this was by far the hardest. It was actually my husband's suggestion to book a night somewhere so I could catch up on some sleep. I discovered with delight how precious this time was. Not just for sleeping, but for reconnecting with all the things I used to love doing. And most important, how to use the time as a health and wellbeing pick-me-up to rejuvenate and fully recharge the batteries.

A night away
to recover from past weeks
to recover myself
to free my self-doubt
to release my responsibility of being a mum
just for one night
to remind myself of who I am
to hold myself,
to sleep deeply
to make choices for me and me alone
and to not feel guilty for it!

Tehla Jane Bower, 6 June 2021

My 'solo night away' concept has inspired my friends and fellow mothers, encouraging them to take the plunge and gift themselves a full night off. It doesn't even have to be twenty-four hours. I've been known to do it in seventeen or eighteen hours, as long as I can get a quality amount of uninterrupted sleep and do at least one nice thing for myself—like take a long bath or lie on the hotel bed reading or journalling.

A rare opportunity requires the planets and the universe to co-conspire to pull it off.

No child sickness. Tick. Partner on board and has no commitments. Tick. Bank balance allows it. Tick. Guilt does not make mother pull out. Extra big TICK. This is what makes it even more vital that you jump at the chance when it comes along.

This is my diary entry from one of the first trips of this kind (Kahlan three, Avah six months):

It's amazing how much difference a day can make. Glen encouraged me to book something last minute to catch up on sleep and this is truly so, so great. I am getting the most out of each minute! It's interesting to observe what choices you make and what you do when you only have your own self-interest to care or worry about. In fact, it can tell you a lot about yourself.

So, I get here and go straight to the gym as I just need to feel the release that comes with sweating it all out— and then feeling like I deserve the reward of swim/spa/relax. It was so fabulous! The next thing I did was fully open up the curtains in my room and sit on the bay window and just look out and watch the people walking by. Just the view—and the feeling of being a bit separate from it all. It was nice.

Then a deep, hot bath with reading and music, followed by room service dinner . The feeling like I could do anything at all is something I haven't felt in so long—I had a bit of a flashback to a time where I truly felt like I was making choices just for me. It was when I was in Malaysia four to five years ago for my MBA study. Two weeks over there just having to look out for myself was so interesting. I learnt so much about myself.

But I have to say motherhood has taught and

*challenged me so much more, particularly since I am
the thinking type and really enjoy my time out.*

*Importantly, it has taught me to be truly grateful for
opportunities like tonight, and to value every minute
by doing all the things I love but can't usually do, like:*

- *read*
- *exercise*
- *yoga*
- *write*
- *sleep!*

*I miss my little girls, but I know I will be better off for
them for it. xx*

Fast forward three years from this first time (Kahlan
six, Avah four), and this is my entry from a night away at a
bed-and-breakfast in the tiny Southern Highlands town of
Bundanoon:

*So, this weekend I am recalibrating I guess—
reminding myself of my true nature and breaking
away from the rat race that I have somehow managed
to get entangled in once again. 'The old Tehla.' Who
is she? And why was I so proud (?) to get back to her?*

*I can't imagine if I didn't get these little openings
to flee the household now and then, to be free and
just be myself—in my own company without all the
attachments of everyday domestic life.*

*I still believe that my ultimate spiritual growth will
be the day when I actually don't have to leave my*

environment to re-centre my wheel. I think it is called 'integration'. But I'm going to give myself a break while the kids are still so young—I bloody need this. And it helps me to be a better mum, too. That I know for sure.

I've overdone the past month or so, and with Avie's elbow/arm situation this week (she dislocated her elbow at the day-care sandpit) I was almost at breaking point with no sleep and no patience left (sorry Dexter—our dog—I think I really took so much out on you this week—and all you really needed was a walk I couldn't give you).

So Yallawallee (a B&B homestead) it is and I'm looking forward to a whole lot of reading and writing, and just hanging out in my own space and company.

Have you had the opportunity to get away for a night on your own? What did you do? Where did you go? How did you maximise your valuable alone time?

Maybe you are feeling the call to get away but just can't quite grasp it in your reach? If you are feeling the elusiveness of a night away, see my prompted suggestions below for some inspiration.

PAUSE PROMPT
FIVE TIPS FOR MANIFESTING
A WELL-DESERVED NIGHT OFF

1. Close your eyes and imagine you are alone without any interruptions.

2. Breathe in for a count of ten, with each count drawing you closer to peace. Feel it deeply.

3. Visualise a place of peace and serenity where you can be truly at one with yourself. Where is this place and what does it look like?

4. Open your journal or notebook and write down and/or draw what you see in your mind's eye.

5. Write down the date of the day you are collecting this intuitive desire. Then record the future date you would like to be in the place of your own choosing for one night. Feel comforted that now you have recorded this desire, you can release your intention to the Universe and allow her to get to work making it happen! Consider it a divine cosmic contract with faith on your side!

Permission Note

I seek courage and commitment to take myself
away for a night alone for the sole purpose of a
well-earned break.

Chapter 22

If I Had Half A Day

"Great opportunities may come once in a lifetime,
but small opportunities surround us every day."

Rick Warren

It is a Monday in early Autumn. The air is crisp, and the sun
is shining bright. My favourite type of weather! My husband
Glen is home from work, releasing me from responsibility—
no school drop-off, no school pick-up, no running around
after school to appointments or after-school activities. No
appointments or deadlines for my own work either, so a
chance to truly let go and get back in touch with my own
personal yearnings.

At the time of writing this, we live within driving distance
of one of the most spiritual, natural environments and cutest
towns in New South Wales: Kangaroo Valley. I have my own
little ritual that I follow each time I sneak away for a bit of
space here. Half a day is all I need to ground myself in these
lush surrounds.

It takes me just over an hour to meander to Kangaroo
Valley by car. Solo, without any background noise, I listen

to music and podcasts of my choosing. The drive itself is magical. Up the steep and winding road through Macquarie Pass National Park, popping out at the quaint little town of Robertson, home of the giant spud ('Big Potato') and filming location for the 1995 movie *'Babe'*. Dropping down through the deep forest chest of Morton National Park and Barrengarry Nature Reserve. Sometimes I grab myself a coffee here as I pass through. On longer trips, I deliberately lose myself in the rabbit warren of dirt roads to the north of the town, in an area known for wild koalas: Kangaloon. *This could have been a gentle calling from my future destiny. In the years to come, our family relocated up north to a koala estate.*

I arrive in the mystical community of Kangaroo Valley and visit the main street to sample the local offerings. I wander around freely and chat to some of the small business owners. The local real estate agent feels compelled to share his entire life story with me (I have that effect on people sometimes) including details of how he and his ex-partner came to live in Kangaroo Valley eighteen years ago, followed by her falling pregnant at forty-six-and-a-half-years old then separating in the years to come. Quite the story, but as I only have an opportunity for half a day's space, I have to leave him to his lucrative property negotiations and hot foot it out of town.

I jump into the car with my iced tea and sandwich and roll out of town onto the Upper Kangaroo Valley Road. A quote by Ralph Waldo Emerson goes something like, *"Adopt the pace of nature: her secret is patience"*. This resonates with me. The drive is so special, especially when the wi-fi and phone reception cuts out. The space I pull over at is equally special. I rationalise this with my inner knowing that Kangaroo Valley is not like anywhere else. It has its own rules and frequency, and it slowly caresses your heart to beat as one with nature.

I drive for about twenty-five minutes until I come to the old community hall where my childhood friend Erin got married. Just across the road is a beaut little spot where I park my car and walk across the rickety, wooden bridge that I love so much. It's so old and rustic and has a structure like it is floating. I check out the river rapids below and admire the pristine, clean, fresh water. Magpies warble and plenty of those dandelion 'Santa Claus' balls of wispy white fluff float around me. I always see so many so often in the most unusual of places. I believe they carry special messages on their fluffy tips that can only be explained through spiritual dimensional footnotes (a story for another book perhaps).

I walk back over the bridge and pull out my yoga mat to spread out on as I eat my lunch slowly and listen to the rushing rapids from the river. Nature really does provide the best music! I am calm and at ease with myself. I feel I have been granted permission to just be. Here and now and unapologetically. I read some pages of my book. On this particular day, I am reading 'The Shallows' by Tim Winton, a marvellous read from the 1980s that ensures the reader never thinks about whales the same way again. A warm smile emerges on my face as I bask in the sunshine. I feel into how proud I am of myself for putting guilt and lists to the side on this day to make proper time out in nature for myself. My soul rejoices, and I enjoy every little minute.

PAUSE PROMPT
DREAMING YOUR OWN HALF DAY
INTO REALITY

As a fellow mother or caregiver, let me ask you a very important question. Try to answer it as honestly as possible!

> 'If you faced half a day to yourself, absolute freedom, no interruptions or responsibilities, no kids or partner, no-one but you, and you could do and go wherever you pleased ... for half a day, where would you go and what would you do?'

This is an interesting question to ponder (and journal about). I can hear some of you rolling your eyes incredulously whilst thinking *half a day free? Yeah, right!* But take it from a mother who has completely transformed her life by claiming her slice of space each and every day. It *is* possible, and you can do it. It doesn't have to be to a place like Kangaroo Valley. It can be anywhere close enough to you to make it happen in half a day!

Permission Note

My day looks different to me when I allow
my dreams to drift into it.

Chapter 23

A Solo Hike
Up A Sacred Mountain

*"It's where we go,
and what we do when we get there,
that tells us who we really are."*

Joyce Carol Oates

In the summer of 2018, the opportunity of a full day to myself plonked directly and divinely into my prospects. We were 'on holidays' back in our hometown. Our girls were still quite young and tired from the Christmas cheer, so the wheels were falling off the holiday cart of harmony. Given I hadn't had much time to myself recently, and we were all getting on each other's nerves, Glen suggested I take a day off to have a break.

Without hesitation, the next day I strapped on my boots, packed my backpack and reserved a full day to immerse myself in a mountain of discovery. Literally.

Mount Gulaga is located in the tiny town of Tilba Tilba on the Far South Coast of New South Wales and holds immense spiritual and cultural heritage value to the local Aboriginal Yuin people. An ancient volcano with an original peak that topped three kilometres in height, the 'mother mountain' now stands at just over 800 metres above sea level. In recent years, the land has been returned to its rightful traditional Aboriginal owners.

A PHYSICAL AND EMOTIONAL CHALLENGE

Mount Gulaga's spiritual presence is felt long before you attempt to climb her. The gravel road leading up to the base of the mountain begins just past Pam's Store in Tilba Tilba. Unfortunately, the store was closed for renovations the day I visited, but I was lucky to bump into the local nursery owner. He was a lovely man called Keith, who kindly shared some of his Aeroguard with me (later I would be *very* grateful for this!) and gave me some handy hints on climbing the mountain. He also requested that I let him know when I returned. He liked to keep a tab on the comings and goings of visitors to ensure everyone returned safely by the day's end. I took note of his phone number and felt comforted in the knowledge I had been included amongst the daily 'headcount'.

As I wandered up the dirt path, taking in the rolling hills of the farms and paddocks, I noticed I was falling under the shadow of the mountain. Dark rain clouds and fog completely shrouded the summit.

Despite being one of the busiest times of year for tourists and visitors to the area, no other walkers were on the track. It was a while before I passed even one person. A young couple in running gear jogged past me after half an hour or so, but it was a good hour or more again before I came across anyone else. I preferred it this way. It was sooooo peaceful. Although there were no other humans, I did not feel alone. A friendly kookaburra flew about fifty metres ahead of me, directing the way, and I came across the tiniest and cutest little brown mouse I have ever laid eyes on! I also felt a deeper presence, whether it was within the trees or right next to me, I could not fully grasp, but I felt it. It was kind of like I was being watched or protected, and I felt safe.

It was a hot day, but the heat subsided the higher I climbed. In fact, the surface of the track was damp and very slippery in parts. I started to think about how hard the trip back down was going to be with my worn-grip shoes. Putting it out of my mind, I focused on the task ahead. To my surprise, about halfway up it became so foggy and misty I couldn't really see in front of me. Visibility was so poor I remember wishing I had one of those hard hats with an inbuilt torch on the front! It poured with rain just as I reached the entrance to the rainforest. To my shock and relief, a pit toilet materialised right when I needed it. I also came across my second human of the trip, an Irish backpacker on his way to the summit. After a few exchanged words, we parted ways, and I gave him some time to go ahead while I reviewed the fascinating collection of information at the small rest stop.

I started my walk through the rainforest track just as the rain started to subside. This track was much narrower and wetter, and riddled with the most beautifully crafted spider webs! I used my walking stick to navigate my way through them, deviating from the path only once or twice to check out some huge moss-covered rocks. The terrain, flora and climate had changed dramatically. I cast my mind back to the previous rest stop bay that informed me of the mountain's mythological relationship with the clouds and rain, and specifically its role as a barometer of the weather in general:

> *"Gulaga is like a weather clock, you can read what the weather is doing or about to do by looking at the mountain ... [it] behaves differently at different times of the day and year."*
>
> **Beryl Brierly, 2006**

My legs felt heavy after the climb, but I forgot all about it as I came across the enormous mossy rocks, trees and fallen logs that inhabited the rainforest walk immediately before the summit. I inhaled the thick air full of mystery and wisdom and—yes, I am admitting to this—I wrapped my arms around the trunk of a huge tree. It had a striking similarity to the one I had imagined from Enid Blyton's 'The Magic Faraway Tree' and I took a moment to breathe in its energy and just exist in this wild and wise area of the mountain. I made a mental note to bring my girls up here when they are older to see the magic for themselves.

The trip down was a lot clearer and brighter and I questioned whether I was walking on the same dark, wet, shadowy track I had come up on! I felt inspired, energised and refreshed by this experience, and I was excited to share my newfound discoveries with Glen and the girls. It didn't cost anything, aside from my time, but it was priceless all the same.

PAUSE PROMPT
NATURAL LANDSCAPE DISCOVERY

What does the natural world around you look like? Do you have any bushland, parks, rock formations, mountains, rivers or oceans close by?

I invite you to rediscover your childhood curiosity by taking a short visit to one of your favourite local natural sites. Take note of every detail large and small. What plants or trees reside on the landscape? What birds or animals can you see? How does it make you feel to be there? Can these feelings help to reconnect you with parts of yourself you might have forgotten about since becoming a mother?

Always say *yes* when offered a chance to have a break! It took me years before I realised how often I was turning offers down because I felt too guilty. Take it from me—the kids get over it, and I have *never* regretted it!

Chapter 24

Spiritual Space

"Spiritual practice is not just sitting and meditating ... Every act, every breath and every step can be practice and can help us to become more ourselves."

Thich Nhat Hanh

At the age of seventeen, I stepped foot into my first yoga class. Almost instantly, it felt like coming home. At such a young age, I did not quite know why. I just knew I needed to keep showing up and dedicating time to this intriguing new interest.

I am so grateful I walked into my teacher Leonard's yoga stretch class that day. It provided the pillars to a lifelong love of physical exploration and soulful, spiritual inquiry. Ten years after my first class, at age twenty-seven, I experienced an incredible visceral connection and 'out of body' awareness that would become my guiding light within my spiritual life. I *felt* it—beyond the pose, beyond my body and within the expansive life force energy surrounding me.

The pose was *Utthita Parsvakonasana* which, translated into English from Sanskrit, is 'Extended Side Angle Pose'. If you have practised any yoga yourself, you might be familiar with this posture or the one most commonly used as its precursor, *Virabhadrasana II* ('Warrior II') pose.

Easing my way into the extended side angle position from the comfort of the sun-drenched, floorboard-filled space off my living room, I gripped my toes, observing how they created a gentle indent in my squishy yoga mat. Turning my right knee out and bending it towards the little toe of the same foot, I could hear my teacher's instructions in my head.

> *"Turn your back foot <u>in</u> thirty degrees and your front foot <u>out</u> ninety degrees ... bring your arms out from your shoulders ... check that you haven't lost your back arm ... bend your front knee towards the little toe of that foot and squash your mat with your feet..."*

Next, I did something I usually don't do. I set my body free, free from instruction, free from questions, free from inhibition. Bending my elbow and placing my right forearm just above my bent right knee, I leaned in and over to the right. Lifting my left arm over my head, I felt the fascial tissue expand across my left side, aligning with the direction of force. I felt strong and alive, not just in the physical sense, but in a new heightened sense that incrementally increased as I turned my head and eyes to gaze up under my top armpit.

A warm energy surrounded me, and I felt that, despite the intensity of the posture, I could stay here forever. I was suspended beyond the physical pose, my breath guiding me deeper and beyond. Even this thread of breath soon evaporated, until I was completely unaffected by the constraints of my physical body. It was how I imagined the mountain yogis to feel after years of solitary meditation in their caves, except I was here—at home—experiencing this mid-posture.

To this day, I can remember every detail of this, my first experience of a true spiritual nature. The realisation that yoga was more of a *feeling* than a *pose*, and that the limitless life-force expansion was something I would return to time and time again.

> This is the same feeling I yearn for when I seek
> a spiritual kind of space in my days as a mother.
> I stroke its essence, I hold its hand, and I know
> I need to completely surrender in order to be in
> its presence.

Do you have any past experiences or vivid memories that can help guide you back to yourself as a mother? A favourite pastime, a delicious meal made with loving intention, an inspiring book, a secret path in nature leading nowhere but at the same time everywhere, a sandy patch at the beach that your younger self would consider her own.

Spiritual space does not have to be sought out on a yoga mat. It can be anywhere the whisperings of your soul can best be heard and felt.

Spiritual space also *looks* different in motherhood. Gone are the days I can reserve my previous ritual of an hour and a half immersion in daily yoga practice without any distractions.

I take what I can. Sometimes that might only be a meditation ten minutes before bed, and that is enough.

I don't believe it is any coincidence that I found my true calling around the same time as motherhood found me. I always knew it held a dear and special place in my life. In many ways, I knew deep down yoga and writing would ultimately lead the way for me. Had I not been so physically and emotionally wrecked, the result of self-neglect and zero sleep for months on end, I would not have had the guts or confidence and courage to step out of my comfort zone and follow this calling. I am forever grateful for the time I hit my 'rock bottom'. If I hadn't been challenged so acutely, I don't think I would have mustered the strength to follow through with the changes I made to my life.

My biggest lesson during this period was to listen to my gut instincts and intuition. There is much to be said about our 'second brain', otherwise known as our enteric nervous system. Science and research are finally catching up with this not-so-fluffy-anymore concept.

To listen in fully, I quietly released what no longer served me and invited in the idea of a   higher purpose in life.

For this I needed a spiritual kind of space,
not much of it, but highly concentrated and
requiring a type of solitude that doesn't come
naturally with the early days of motherhood.

A simple set of conditions can make this possible. I need to be:

1. Alone,
2. In a quiet and peaceful setting
3. Temporarily relinquished from the immediate responsibilities of motherhood

I documented an example of when I spontaneously claimed a slice of spiritual space at my local Buddhist temple in my journal at the time (Kahlan two, Avah six months):

When I sit out here at the Temple, I feel like I could solve all of my issues at once, strip them away from me one by one, and wrap myself in a calm and peaceful warmth. It's nice to sit here and observe myself, my feelings and thoughts, like I'm looking at myself from outside of my body. Today it is the anxiety of leaving Avah, the guilt of leaving her when sick, the bloatedness and exhaustion that I haven't been able to shake all week, the cold weather and the comfort of my winter clothes and boots. And gradually, sip by sip of my tea, the release and letting go of each of these discomforts.

I often choose to stroll around the temple grounds whenever I visit this beautiful place. It is the best form of 'walking meditation' I have been able to directly experience in my spiritual journey so far. I have a little ritual where I start on the southern side of the grounds and follow the pathway up the steep incline to a small observation deck with a wooden chair. I linger here as long as I feel necessary and breathe in the stillness and calm. Sweeping views capture our two sacred mountains, Djera (Mount Keira) and Djembla (Mount Kembla), and I believe it is no coincidence that the original developers of this majestic temple chose this exact geographic location between both mountains to erect its shrines and associated grounds. I am in awe of the meticulous and tedious efforts used to create this harmonious, peaceful, spiritual environment. I want to bottle it and take it home with me.

I continue along the path and over a small bridge and make my way up towards the 'Gratitude Bell'. Visitors can manually activate this huge gong-like structure of devotion, resulting in a deep penetrating vibratory sound that echoes across the entire landscape. It always reminds me of the silent meditation retreat I participated in on these same grounds. We started the day early at 5.00 am at the Main Shrine with the 'gong' ceremony led by the monks who resided there. If I close my eyes, I can still smell the incense offerings at the shrine entrance.

PAUSE PROMPT
SPIRITUAL PONDERINGS:
POETRY IN ACTION

"For all the grasses rustling at your feet
And every flaming star that glitters high
Above you, close up and meet
In you: The Eternal I."

Jane Goodall, extract from *'The Old Wisdom'* in
'Reason for Hope: A Spiritual Journey'

Permission Note

A familiar and powerful life-force
energy surrounds me.
It encourages me to reconnect with the parts
of myself I have forgotten about.

Chapter 25

Space Holding

"The circles of women around us
Weave invisible nets of love that
Carry us when we're weak
And sing with us when we're strong."

Sark

Connecting with other mothers and women plays an important role in a mother's health and wellbeing. Sometimes we resist support after experiencing undue judgement and criticism from other mothers (why oh, why!), but don't let this be a hindrance to finding comfort and reassurance from those women and fellow mothers who lift you up and notice you when you feel unnoticed.

According to psychologist Sheryl Ziegler, *'the problem with no name'* coined by Betty Friedan[15] in the 1960s is still well and truly alive and contributing to patterns of miserable mothers. *A Mother's Space* has largely focused on seeking out quiet pockets of stillness and solitude for the benefit of a mother's wellbeing and spiritual growth. However, this personal journey can be complemented with meaningful connections with other like-minded women and holding space for those mothers who might be struggling to access their own private sanctuary.

Holding space: *being present with someone, without judgement*

The women and other mothers who hold space for you may not play a regular role in your social calendar. They might even be a stranger, or a friend of a friend, a colleague or a mother from your mother's group. They might be someone you call on when you're feeling overwhelmed or feel the need to get out to a gym class or a yoga session. They might be your best friends from primary school.

I would like to share with you two examples of how I've held space for other mothers, both of whom were strangers to me prior to our meeting.

The first was a twenty-two-year-old single mother whose then three-year-old was in my eldest's dance class. We started chatting in the 'mum's waiting area' while the girls danced. At first, I assumed we had zip in common. In fact, I remember at one point in the half-hour wait period thinking (wishing) we would just stop talking so I could close my eyes and enjoy the break and peace on my own. But, as we talked, I realised that although she was twelve years younger than me, as a fellow mother of two, she faced the same experiences, obstacles and feelings I did.

The conversation dived deeper. She opened up to me about how she wished she had waited longer before having kids, how old it made her feel and how she *loved* being back to work as it was a much-needed break from the kids. Her older sister, who was yet to have children of her own, had recently demanded a 'kid-free night' for a family event that she had no choice but to take her kids to. She shared how isolating that made her feel and how trapped she felt in her own life. But also, how lucky she felt to be the sole parent of her two beautiful kids, born fourteen months apart, whom she adored. She thanked me profusely for listening to her spew out her life story and apologised for taking up my time. I had sat patiently and quietly, nodding my head and offering genuine advice and feedback where I felt called to. Just like a spontaneous smile from a stranger in the street, she felt relieved, uplifted and grateful for my support during this half-hour share session from one mother to another.

This is often all that is required to hold space for another mother.

My second encounter was when my eldest girl was at preschool. One particular morning after dropping her off, I was on the brink of tears because my own daughter had *bitten* me on the arm, frustrated I was leaving her. I fought back the stinging sensation in the corners of my eyes and turned to witness a little Chinese girl screaming after her own mother as she tried to escape quickly and briskly (don't we all!). I bumped into the quiet, reserved mother in the carpark and realised her eyes were all welled up with tears. She turned to brush them away, but they just kept pouring out. I felt I had no choice but to hug the poor woman and comfort her with words I probably should have used for myself that day. I held space for that mother without judgement and assured her it was okay to let her guard down from time to time. We may feel like it some days, but we are not superhuman!

These two encounters revealed to me that no matter if we are a twenty-two-year-old single mother, a thirty-something-year-old, broken-English speaking Chinese mother or a Caucasian career woman and mother, we all experience the same type of daily hardships and triumphs that we otherwise wouldn't in the parent-less versions of ourselves. We are all fighting some battle or experiencing some crisis from time to time. We should never disregard the positive impact we can have on a fellow mother in need by the simple act of reaching out and listening or empathising.

It could be the difference between a breakdown and a breakthrough.

PAUSE PROMPT
REACH OUT

Today I encourage you to pause, not just for yourself, but for the fellow mothers who surround you every day. The mum in line at the coffee shop juggling a double pram and a toddler tantrum. The school mum struggling to get her children to drop-off on time, after being up all night with her newborn. The mother at the supermarket or Kmart at 9.00 pm just to give herself a break from the relentless routine. The mum who arrives late to work to be greeted by the disapproving eyes of her co-workers.

Pause for just a moment and take in their energy and situation and give that mother a warm smile. Ask if you can help her out if she's struggling. Try not to ignore her with the justification that it's none of your business, or that you are too busy to truly double-check if she's okay. If you are questioning it, she's probably not.

Reach out, check in, smile, and you might be surprised at how much you can turn her morning around.

Permission Note

I am grateful to those who reach out to me reassuringly in my greatest moments of need.

EPILOGUE AND INTEGRATION

I drove up the long and winding road with a whiff of whimsy and an inner call to completion. Keeping me to task as it twisted and turned, the road appeared unsettled by the natural environment in which it found itself planted firmly and permanently. Smiling to myself, it reminded me of my younger self some eleven-and-a-half-years ago, a fresh young mother trying earnestly to navigate her way in this new chapter of her life. Learning to lean into her mistakes whilst simultaneously surrendering to the tender whisperings of her soul. Letting go of all prior expectations she had of herself and the baby she had recently birthed. Allowing space for new gifts to grow and places within herself to discover.

Pulling into my destination for the night, the gravel growled under my car tyres as I slowed to a stop. I had been on the road for half the day, and it was a relief to stretch my legs and breathe in the crisp cold air offered by the late autumn afternoon. In this tiny town of Tenterfield, I would write this final chapter of *A Mother's Space: Permission to Pause.* I mused at how appropriate this was, closing off the book with a long stretch of well-deserved space in a cute cosy town.

My writing cave was a tidy but worn motel room, well beyond its heyday but comfortable enough. It revealed its magic when I noticed two old churches outside the stern end of the room, glowing in the sunset and instilling my heart with hope. There was an uncanny sense of a divine championing of my journey, as if the churches were cheering me on and encouraging me further. The pink rose hues of the intricate stained-glass windows became my guiding light over the coming days, and I am so grateful for their inspiration.

My mind meandered to my girls, so grown up at ages eleven and nine, finding their place in this world and continuing to surprise me every day. It was just over a year ago that our family of four sold our house of seventeen years, taking with us all of its memories, both good and not-so-good, and leaving behind everything familiar. An up-rooting. A fresh start. A new beginning for us all.

Re-planting ourselves in a friendly coastal community on the Far North Coast of NSW, we knew not one other person, but we instantly felt we belonged. We started to build our networks again, helping first with the infamous 2022 flooding in the Northern Rivers, and supporting our girls as they found their way into a new school life and friendships.

The slower pace has served us well and has made way for new chapters of growth and space in our lives.

I am the first to admit I am not immune to feelings of guilt, frustration or irritations at not having my 'me time' on certain days, but the intensity of these feelings is far less destructive to my health. I still struggle with balancing my auto-immune disease, as well as Premenstrual Dysphoric Disorder (PMDD) and chronic Temporomandibular Joint Dysfunction (TMJ), but my healing trajectory is heading in the right direction.

Maybe I might write a book about that one day too!

My relationship with my husband has experienced the biggest shift, to the point now where he has become my biggest advocate for my alone time and champion of this book.

He gets it. He gets *me*. I'm so grateful to have his support and have him by my side in this, the greatest roles we will ever take on in our lifetimes—being mother and father to our two beautiful girls.

A lot has happened during this period of 'space-seeking'. I have grown more confident, assured and justified in seeking out this time unapologetically, knowing I truly deserve it.

My hope is this book can be your own personal cheer squad, encouraging you forward and reminding you of your worthiness for personal, private space reserved *just for you*, in your darkest moments of desperation and brightest moments of exaltation. That you can look at this book or even simply hold it in your hands and feel empowered to take your first, second or third step into your own space-seeking journey.

I am that invisible guide at your side, lifting you up and saluting you for honouring your yearnings, no matter how brief they are or how much of your energy it takes to claim them. I look forward to witnessing and hearing all about your own transition into a purposeful space-filled life as a calmer, stronger and more aligned version of your incredible self.

All my love,

Tehla Jane xx

"The magic of claiming space is the canny but whimsical ability to weave it in so it cannot be found—by anyone but you."

NOTES

1   Bort, Julie & Pflock, Aviva & Renner, Devra (2005). *'Mommy Guilt: Learn to Worry Less, Focus on What Matters Most, and Raise Happier Kids.'* American Management Association, New York

2   Australian Institute of Family Studies (2016) *'Mothers still do lion's share of housework'*, Research Summary, May. Mothers still do the lion's share of housework | Australian Institute of Family Studies (aifs. gov.au)

3   *'Wellbeing of Mothers May 2019'*, Focus on the Family Singapore Ltd, www.family.org.sg

4   Bower, T. (2016) *'We're Living in a Society of Head-Down 'Smombies' & It's Making Us Miserable'*, Elephant Journal. We're Living in a Society of Head-Down "Smombies" & it's Making us Miserable. | Elephant Journal

5   Lishman, M. in Merrillees, L. (2016) *'Psychologists scramble to keep up with social media addiction'*, ABC News. Psychologists scramble to keep up with growing social media addiction - ABC News

6   (2020) *'Digital Detox: I've been off social media for 12 days and this is what I've learned...'* https://youtu.be/fhEuTswXONw

7   Williams & Bargh (2008) *'Experiencing Physical Warmth Promotes Interpersonal Warmth'*, Science, Oct 24: 332 (5901): 606-607

8   Venerable Master Hsing Yun (2014) *'Buddhism and the Tea Ceremony'*, Buddhism and the Tea Ceremony - Tibetan Buddhist Encyclopedia

9   Moss, T. in Priestley, A. (2015) *'Forget having it all and try this instead',* Women's Agenda. Tara Moss: Forget having it all and try this instead | Women's Agenda (womensagenda.com.au)

10 Morin, A. (2018) *'5 ways solitude can make you more successful'*, Inc. 5 Ways Solitude Can Make You More Successful, Backed By Science Inc.com

11 Gemmell, N. in Powers, R (2015) *'Motherhood & Creativity: The Divided Heart'*, Affirm Press, Mulgrave.

12 Postpartum Insomnia: Sleep Tips for New Moms | Sleep Foundation

13 The Dalai Lama, Arianna Huffington Interview: His Holiness Discusses Compassion, Science, Religion And Sleep (VIDEO) HuffPost Religion

14 Sleep Duration and All-Cause Mortality: A Systematic Review and Meta-Analysis of Prospective Studies - PMC (nih.gov)

15 Friedan, B. (1963) *'The Feminine Mystique'*, Penguin, UK.

ACKNOWLEDGEMENTS

The writing of this book has been a cathartic, emotional, exhilarating and humbling experience. Eleven years of scribbling, musing, starting over and challenging the dichotomy of doubt and belief in myself. Fortunately, the universe conscripted the right people at precisely the right time in my path to ensure the energy of this book would radiate out from its modest beginnings.

To the brilliant Amy Molloy, for helping me discover my writing voice, encouraging me to dig deep and share 'the story that only you can tell'. Thank you for your belief and encouragement in the times when I most needed it. This book would not have happened without you. To Gabby Bernstein for her perfectly aligned writing course offerings that inspired the title of this book and ensured that I 'got out of my own way'. To Phil Cotterell for your honest advice and industry insight that helped steer me in the right direction. To Linda Sivertsen and the Beautiful Writers Community—thank you for your guidance and gentle encouragement to keep going.

To the Hay House Writing Community for your support of my book concept and hook, and for helping me create a book proposal that would turn my dream into a reality.

To my publisher Natasha Gilmour, whom I could dedicate an entire book of acknowledgement to, for your unwavering faith in me and my manuscript. We have traversed many moon cycles with 'the woman' and the story and I cannot imagine anyone else more capable of bringing this book into the world than you and the kind press. To Christa Moffitt for patiently creating the divine cover design and Rananda Rich for your invaluable editing prowess. What a team you are.

To the man who had my back throughout this entire process, even though he knew the content was spotlighting some of our darker moments. He understood how important it was, not only to me but to all the other mothers out there who needed a reassuring tap on the shoulder that it is okay to make space for themselves. Glen Bower—I love you endlessly, and I am so grateful for your unconditional love and support.

To my best friend Danielle, for being there and cheering me on with this book since day one, as I read chapter drafts to you over the phone. Thank you for laughing and crying with me through our ups and downs as we navigated early motherhood together. To Jess DeAngelis, for your incredible ongoing support and for whipping up selfie videos from your kitchen cupboard in lightning speed. Kate Pascoe, Leia Thompson, Shenny Mackie, Natali Lazaroski, Jeni Abraham, and my sisters Carly and Amie for years of listening to update after update about my latest title, chapter or story idea. My 'Potty Mammas' Jac, Charlie, Janet, Megan and Chloe—I'm so happy you all came into my life. And to all the mothers out there reading this—I wrote this book for you, and I dedicate it to you.

To Milina Opsenica and Rebecca Cossio for the last-minute photoshoot session and all the magic you worked to make it perfect.

To my parents, Toni and Peter, for encouraging my reading from an early age and always having the bookshelves overflowing with new and interesting titles.

This book has been written across many stages and phases of motherhood—featuring two lead characters! My girls, Kahlan and Avah, my biggest achievements in life so far and my greatest teachers and inspiration. Thank you for choosing me in this lifetime. We have learned so much together and I am a better version of myself because of you both. You have challenged me to make courageous changes in my life that I never would have thought possible. Mummy loves you both more than any word I could ever hope to write.

ABOUT THE AUTHOR

Tehla Jane Bower is a mother of two, writer, spiritual teacher and founder of The Crystal Healing Room in Far North NSW. Her early career in communications and community relations shaped her multidimensional approach to life and work. Following her transition into motherhood, Tehla rekindled her spiritual purpose and writing passion, with her work featured in esteemed platforms such as Australian Yoga Life Magazine, Mamamia, and Elephant Journal. Her first published work of poetry was at age seventeen, titled 'Quiet Search'. A Mother's Space: Permission to Pause reflects her genuine voice and commitment to self-discovery.

Tehla is a registered Yoga Teacher, Certified Crystal Energy Guide, Crystal Awakening Practitioner and Certified Angel Guide. Academically she holds a Bachelor of Arts (Distinction) and MBA (Distinction/Valedictorian).

Tehla loves sharing her passion and voice with others, facilitating events, workshops and retreats, predominantly for women and mothers. She also offers a gentle fusion of 1:1 healing, meditation and guidance from her home-based sanctuary. She lives in Pottsville, Australia with her husband and two young girls.

www.tehlajane.com
@tehla_jane